FROM HOUSE TO WEALTH

How Smart Homeowners Build Equity, Avoid Costly Mistakes, and Turn Their Home Into a Financial Asset

JASON GELIOS

Disclaimer
The information contained in this book is provided for general informational purposes only. It is not intended to be, and should not be construed as, financial, legal, or professional advice. Readers should consult with a qualified financial advisor, attorney, or other appropriate professional before making any decisions based on the content presented. The author and publisher assume no responsibility or liability for any actions taken by readers based on the information in this book.

Book design by Jason Gelios
Proofread by Patricia Gordon
ISBN: 979-8-234-12979-6

Also By Jason Gelios:

Think Like a Realtor: New Edition

Beating The Force Of Average

The Seniors Guide To Buying and Selling a Home

From House To Wealth

TABLE OF CONTENTS

SECTION 7: The Mindset and Habits of Successful Home Wealth Builders

SECTION 8: When Owning a Home Doesn't Lead To Wealth

CONCLUSION

INTRODUCTION

WHY YOUR HOME IS ONE OF YOUR GREATEST WEALTH-BUILDING TOOLS.

Owning a home forces you to do something most people struggle with: consistently build equity while benefiting from appreciation and leverage.

Here's the reality:

1. You're paying yourself every month (whether you realize it or not)

Part of your mortgage payment goes toward principal. That's not an expense, it's forced savings. When you pay rent, it's gone forever.

2. Leverage multiplies your gains.

You might put 15-20% down, but you control 100% of the asset. If your home goes up 5% in value, your actual return on your cash is much higher.

3. Appreciation works quietly in the background.

Real estate typically rises over time. Not in a straight line, but over decades, it trends up. That growth stacks on top of your equity paydown.

4. Inflation works in your favor.

Your mortgage payment stays relatively stable, if you have a fixed rate. Meanwhile rents and home values rise.

5. There are tax advantages.
Mortgage interest, property taxes, capital gains exclusions can all play in your favor if you understand them. *Disclosure: Always seek professional advice from a CPA or tax professional.*

6. It's one of the few assets people actually hold long-term.
A home only becomes a great wealth-building tool if you:

- Don't overpay.
- Stay long enough (5 plus years).
- Choose a solid location.
- Manage your financing strategy wisely.

Otherwise, it can just as easily stall your financial growth.

UNDERSTANDING EQUITY IN SIMPLE TERMS
Since we will be exploring the topic of equity multiple times in the upcoming sections, I will share with you a brief definition of what equity is in simple terms.

Equity = Home Value - Mortgage Balance

For example, if your home value is $250,000, and you have a mortgage balance of $100,000, your equity is $150,000.

HOW SMALL DECISIONS CREATE LONG-TERM FINANCIAL IMPACT

Most homeowners obsess over the “big decisions” such as purchase price, interest rate, and timing the market. That’s not where the real money is made or lost. It’s the small, repeatable decisions that quietly compound over the years.

Here’s how it plays out:

1. Making one extra payment a year

One extra mortgage payment annually doesn’t feel life changing.

But over time:

- You shave years off your loan.
- You save tens of thousands of dollars in interest.
- You build equity faster without increasing your lifestyle cost.

A small sacrifice means massive long-term leverage.

2. Rounding up your payment

Let’s say your mortgage payment is $1,842 and you pay $2,000 instead:

- That extra $158 a month goes straight to principal.
- You accelerate payoff without feeling a major hit.
- Over 10-20 years, this stacks into serious equity.

Discipline, not income, does the heavy lifting.

3. Choosing a slightly lower purchase price

Buying a home $20-30,000 under your maximum budget:

- Lowers your monthly payment.
- Reduces your total interest paid over time.
- Gives you flexibility.

Most people stretch. The smarter move is to create margin.

4. Handling small repairs early

Ignoring a $300 issue can turn into a $5,000 problem.

Homeownership rewards:

- Preventative maintenance
- Quick decision-making
- Not procrastinating on problems

This protects your equity.

5. Refinancing strategically without emotion

People either:

- Refinance too often (resetting their loan).
- Or never refinance when it actually makes sense.

A small rate improvement at the right time can save you thousands, or free up cash flow to reinvest elsewhere. The key is strategy, not reaction.

6. Consistent, modest upgrades

This is where I see home sellers make the biggest mistake. You don't need HGTV level upgrades.

Small improvements over time:
1. Keep your home competitive in the market.
2. Protect resale value.
3. Increase livability.

Think paint, fixtures, and landscaping.

7. "Staying put" longer
This is the quiet killer, or builder, of wealth.

Every time you move:
- You reset transaction costs.
- You pay commissions, fees, and moving costs.
- You restart amortization.

"Staying put" just a few extra years can outperform trying to "upgrade" too often.

Wealth in real estate isn't built through one perfect decision. It's built through consistency, patience, and small, smart choices repeated over time. Most people look for a breakthrough moment. In reality, it's the boring decisions that win.

SECTION 1
BUYING YOUR HOME THE RIGHT WAY

1.1 Buying With Wealth In Mind

When purchasing a home, it's important to buy not only with resale in mind, but long-term wealth. Even if you plan on staying in the home for decades, having this wealth mindset will better your financial situation and gain wealth over the years. You never want to buy based on emotion, and then try to justify it later.

Here are some tips you can use to develop a wealth mindset:

1. Stop thinking "dream home". Think "strategic asset"
Your first (or next) home shouldn't just feel right, it should perform for you.

Ask yourself:
- Will this home be easy to resell?
- Would someone else rent this if needed?
- Is demand in my area growing?

If you can't confidently answer yes to these questions, you're buying a liability dressed up as a lifestyle choice.

2. Buy below your ceiling, not at it

It's been my experience that banks approve you for way more than you should spend.

If you max out your budget:

- You kill your ability to invest elsewhere.
- You become house-poor.
- You lose flexibility when opportunities show up.

Wealthy buyers leave margin. That margin turns into:

- Investments.
- Upgrades that add value.
- Peace of mind.

3. Location isn't everything

Many people say "location, location, location". That's lazy thinking.

What matters more:

- Is the area improving?
- Are jobs and development moving in?
- Are prices still reasonable relative to nearby areas?

You make money buying where things are going, not where they already peaked.

4. Look for boring advantages

The flashy house rarely makes financial sense.

The winners are:

- Slightly outdated homes in great areas.
- Homes with functional layouts.
- Properties that need cosmetic, not structural, work.

You're buying equity opportunity, not someone else's finished project.

5. Think exit strategy before you buy

Most people never ask how will this home make me money down the road?

You should know:

- What kind of buyer will want this home in 5-10 years.
- Whether it can be converted to a rental.
- What improvements actually increase value.

Your gambling if you don't have an exit strategy.

6. Use your home as a stepping stone-not a final destination.

Wealthy homeowners don't marry their first house.

They:

- Build equity.
- Move up strategically.
- Repeat the process.

Your goal isn't to arrive. It's to progress. If it looks good and drains you every month, it's not an asset.

THINKING BEYOND "MONTHLY PAYMENT"

If you only focus on the mortgage payment, you're thinking like a consumer. If you think beyond it, you start thinking like an owner building leverage and long-term wealth.

Here's the reality you need to internalize:

1. The mortgage payment is just the entry fee

Your payment is not the cost of the house. It's the cost of financing the house.

What actually matters:

- How fast you build equity.
- How long you hold the asset.
- What the property becomes worth over time.

Two people can have the same payment and end up with completely different financial outcomes.

2. Equity is the real game

Every payment does two things:

- Pays interest
- Builds equity

Your job isn't just to afford the payment. Your job is to accelerate equity growth strategically.

That means:

- Buying in areas with strong appreciation potential.
- Not overpaying just to win a house.
- Making smart improvements that actually add value.

3. The hidden costs will expose you if you ignore them
Most people get blindsided because they only look at principal and interest.

You need to account for:

- Property taxes possibly going up.
- Insurance rising.
- Maintenance (about 1-2% of your home value).
- Utilities.
- Opportunity cost (What else could your money be doing).

If you're tight on cash after buying, you didn't buy smart. You bought emotional.

4. Time in the market beats timing the market
People obsess over rates and timing. What actually builds wealth is holding the property a long time, and letting appreciation amortization compounding do their work. Short-term thinking kills returns. Real estate rewards patience, not perfection.

5. Your exit strategy matters more than your purchase
I tell homebuyers often it's important to think of resale, even if you plan on being in the home for years. Most buyers have zero plan beyond buy the house.

Before you buy, you should know:

- Will this be a rental later?
- Is this a 5-year home or a 15-year hold?
- Does this property appeal to future buyers?

If you don't know your exit, you are guessing-not investing.

6. Lifestyle vs wealth tradeoff
Bigger, newer, nicer = higher monthly burn
More modest, strategic = more wealth flexibility

Thinking beyond the mortgage payment means asking:

- What is this house going to do for me financially over 5-10 years?
- Is this asset helping me build leverage, or just draining cash?
- Am I buying a home, or buying a future problem?

WHY PURCHASE PRICE MATTERS MORE THAN PEOPLE THINK

When I work with home buyers, there is one common thread that occurs, emotions happen. It can be emotional looking at multiple homes and not finding the 'right one'. But then it happens, the 'right one' appears. Then emotion kicks in. The buyer(s) really want the house and will let their guard down during negotiations revealing how bad they want the home. While this is understandable, it's important to check emotions at the door.

Most people fixate on the monthly payment too. That's a mistake. The purchase price quitely controls almost everything that happens financially after you buy.

Here's why it matters more than people think:

1. It locks in your long-term cost
Even small differences in price compound over time. An extra $25,000 doesn't just mean a slightly higher payment, it means tens of thousands of dollars more in interest over the life of the loan.

2. It determines your wealth-building speed
Your equity growth is tied to what you paid. Overpay, and you start behind. Buy right, and appreciation works harder for you from day one.

3. It impacts your flexibility
A higher purchase price means a higher payment, taxes, and insurance. That reduces your margins. Less margin means fewer options if income changes, opportunities come up, or you want to invest elsewhere.

4. It raises your risk exposure
If the market softens, the people who stretched on price feel it first. Buying at or above peak value leaves you vulnerable to being stuck or even underwater.

5. It affects your exit strategy
Your future resale depends on today's price. Overpaying narrows your buyer pool later and can limit your ability to move when you want.

The purchase price isn't just a number. It's the foundation of your financial outcome. Most people negotiate monthly payment. The smart ones negotiate price relentlessly because that's where the real leverage is.

THE DANGER OF EMOTIONAL BUYING

Emotionally buying a house is one of the fastest ways to quietly sabotage your finances. Which most people don't realize until years later.

Here's the reality:

1. You overpay and justify it

When you fall in love with a house, logic takes a back seat. You start stretching telling yourself 'it's only an extra 20k', or 'we'll make it work'. That mindset turns you into an easy win for the seller. You stop negotiating hard, and you often pay above market value.

2. You ignore red flags

Emotion blinds you to problems you'd normally question.

Things like:

- Bad layout
- Location issues
- Needed repairs
- Resale concerns

You don't buy the house, you buy the feeling. Feelings don't show up on an inspection report, but the problems will.

3. You blow past your real budget
This is a dangerous thing to do.

You start focusing on the monthly payment instead of total cost:
- Higher taxes
- Insurance costs
- Maintenance
- Furnishing to match the house

Now you're house-rich and cash-poor. That stress creeps into every part of your life.

4. You reduce your future options
A home should support your life, not trap it.

Overextending means:
- Less ability to invest.
- Less flexibility if income drops.
- Harder to move when life changes.

You've basically handcuffed your future to a decision driven by a moment.

5. You mistake consumption for investment
This is the biggest lie people tell themselves. They say "it's an investment". A primary home can build wealth, but overpaying for an emotional purchase kills that advantage. Appreciation doesn't bail out bad buying decisions as often as people think.

Here is what disciplined buyers do:

- Set a hard ceiling before shopping for a house-and don't move it.
- Be willing to walk away, even from 'the one'.
- Treat negotiation like a business transaction, not a personal win.

Ask: Would I still buy this if I felt neutral about it?

If the answer is no, you're not buying smart, you're buying emotional.

1.2 Choosing The Right Property

It may seem like choosing the right property means finding "the perfect one". But what it really means is making a decision that won't quietly hurt you financially or emotionally 2-5 years from date of purchase. Most people get this wrong because they chase feelings instead of outcomes.

Here's how to approach it like someone who wins long-term:

1. Start with your exit strategy before you buy

Ask yourself these questions:

- Will I sell in 3-5 years?
- Could this become a rental?
- Is this a forever home?

If you don't think about resale before you buy, you'll pay for it later. Prioritize a desirable location, normal floor plan, and broad appeal i.e. 3 bed, 2 bath tends to be the most popular.

2. Location is more important than the house
You can upgrade a house. You can't fix:
- A busy road.
- Bad surrounding homes.
- Noise pollution.
- Poor school districts.

Buy the worst house in a good area, not the best house in a bad one.

3. Don't let emotion override math
That staged kitchen? It's designed to disarm you.

Before you send over an offer, force yourself to evaluate:
- Price vs recent comparable sales.
- Cost of repairs.
- Monthly payment vs your real budget.

People don't lose money on homes because of bad luck. They lose it because they overpaid emotionally.

4. Know your non-negotiables
When I first meet with home buyers, I ask them what there "must-have's" are. It's a good idea to pick 3-5 things you will not compromise on.

These could be:
- Location radius
- Number of bedrooms

- Garage/Basement
- Commute time

If your wish list consists of 20 items, that could cause decision paralysis or bad decisions.

5. Think beyond the mortgage payment
The payment is just the surface.

You also need to factor:
- Property taxes
- Insurance
- Maintenance (1-2% of home value annually)
- Utilities

If you're stretching to afford the mortgage, you definitely can't afford the house.

6. Inspect the home like a skeptic
Remember, you are buying a structure, not just a house. Watch for the age of the roof, foundation issues, HVAC condition and any plumbing or electrical issues.

7. Buy for your life-not someone elses
Don't buy:
- What social media tells you.
- What your parents think you should buy.
- What your agent is excited about.

Buy based on:
- Your income stability.

- Your lifestyle.
- Your long-term goals.

A smart home purchase does three things:
1. Fit's your life today
2. Protects your downside
3. Positions you to build equity over time

Most buyers only focus on #1, which is why they regret it later.

LOCATION VS HOUSE CONDITION

Location should almost always outweigh condition when buying a home. You can improve a property over time, but you can't change where it sits. A well-maintained home in a weak location can struggle to appreciate and limit your long-term equity growth. On the other hand, a home that needs work in a strong location gives you the opportunity to build equity through improvements while benefiting from the area's overall demand and appreciation.

You can change the condition of a home.

You can not change the location of a home.

Why does location matter?

A great location gives you:
- Stronger appreciation over time.
- Better resale demand.

- Protection in down markets.
- Access to better schools, jobs, and amenities.

A bad location:
- Makes your home harder to sell.
- Get's exposed fast when the market shifts

When does condition matter more?

Condition matters only when:
- The home is so rough it scares off financing.
- Repairs exceed your budget or skillset.
- It's priced incorrectly relative to needed work.

Take note of this:
Buy the ugliest house in the best neighborhood.

WHAT ACTUALLY APPRECIATES VS WHAT DOESN'T
When you buy a home, you're either buying an asset that works for you or a liability disguised as one. Most people don't know the difference until it's too late.

Let's explore what actually appreciates:
1. Location, location, location
- Good school districts
- Low crime
- Walkability, proximity to jobs, downtowns
- Limited land/high demand areas

2. Land and lot characteristics
- Larger lots

- Privacy i.e. backing up to woods/water
- Corner lots
- Usable land

3. Functional square footage
- Open layouts
- Extra bedrooms and bathrooms
- Finished basements
- Home office space

4. School district and community growth
- Strong schools = buyer demand
- Growing areas i.e. new jobs, infrastructure

5. Well-done renovations
- Updated kitchens and bathrooms
- Neutral, timeless finishes
- Quality materials
- Renovations should appeal to buyers, not your personal taste.

We just explored what appreciates a home, now let's explore what doesn't:

1. Over-improving for the neighborhood
- Putting a $150,000 kitchen in a $300,000 neighborhood
- Being the most expensive home on the block

2. Highly personalized or trendy finishes
- Bold colors, custom themes
- Ultra-trendy finishes that age fast

3. Poor layouts
- Tiny kitchens
- Awkward room flow
- Too many or too few bedrooms for the price range

4. External Obsolescense
- Busy roads
- Power lines
- Commercial buildings
- Future development

5. Maintenance neglect
- Roof, HVAC, windows, foundation issues
- Deferred maintenance compounds fast

Most buyers focus on granite vs quartz, neutral paint colors, and cosmetic stuff. Even smarter buyers focus on location, the land, layout, and long-term demand.

RED FLAGS THAT KILL FUTURE VALUE

Not everything you do to a home adds value. Matter of fact, there are things that can actually hurt your value. From choosing the wrong updates to overrenovating your home above what the area commands.

Let's explore the things that can hurt home value:

1. Poor first impression (curb appeal)

If the outside feels neglected, buyers assume the inside is worse.

- Peeling paint, cracked driveway, overgrown landscaping
- Old or damaged roof
- Outdated front door or garage door

This is where buyers start subtracting money before they even walk in.

2. Deferred maintenance

This is the silent killer of value.

- Leaky faucets, stained ceilings, cracked walls
- HVAC, plumbing, or electrical issues
- Evidence of "quick fixes" instead of proper repairs

Buyers will think: "What else is wrong that I can't see?" That fear turns into low offers or even no offers.

3. Odors

You cannot out-negotatiate a bad smell.

- Smoke, pets, mildew, heavy cooking odors

Smell triggers emotion instantly. Emotion drives decisions. A bad smell leads to lower perceived value.

4. Outdated interiors

Not everything needs to be brand new. But obvious dated features hurt.

- Old kitchen, (oak cabinets, laminate counters)
- Worn carpet, outdated tile
- Popcorn ceilings

Buyers don't just see outdated. They calculate renovation costs and subtract more than it actually costs.

5. Poor layout or functionality

This is harder and more expensive to fix.

- Choppy floor plans
- Too many small rooms
- Lack of storage
- Awkward additions

You can't stage your way out of a bad layout.

6. DIY work done badly

This one destroys trust instantly.

- Uneven tile, sloppy paint, exposed wiring
- Non-permitted renovations

Buyers assume they'll have to redo everything. Not to mention permits, inspections and legal issues.

7. Water damage or mold

- Basement moisture
- Mold spots
- Foundation cracks

Even small signs can scare buyers into walking away completely.

8. Bad lighting

Dark homes feel smaller and less valuable.

- Dim rooms
- Heavy window coverings

- Outdated light fixtures

Light = perceived space and cleanliness.

9. Location-based issues

You can't fix this, but it still matters.

- Busy roads
- Nearby commercial or industrial properties
- Poorly perceived school districts

You don't control it, but you must price accordingly or you'll sit on the market.

10. Overpricing

This is probably the biggest mistake I see.

- Sitting too long on the market
- Price reductions that signal desperation

The longer a home sit's on the market, the more buyers feel something is wrong.

Value isn't about the house. It's about buyer confidence. Every red flag introduces doubt, which leads to a discounted offer price.

1.3 Negotiation And Timing

WHY OVERPAYING CRUSHES LONG-TERM EQUITY

They say you make your money when you purchase a home. There is truth behind this statement. Overpaying doesn't just hurt at closing, it quietly limits your financial upside for years.

When you pay above a home's true market value, you start with little to no equity. That means it takes longer for appreciation to "catch up" to what you paid, especially if the market slows or levels off. In the meantime, you're still paying interest on that inflated price, which compounds the cost over time.

It also reduces your flexibility. If you need to sell sooner than expected, you could be stuck breaking even, or worse, bringing money to the table. Even in a rising market, your return is weaker compared to someone who bought at a fair price.

In short, the deal you make on day one heavily determines how much wealth that home can actually build.

MARKET TIMING VS PERSONAL TIMING

Most buyers and sellers believe they can time the market perfectly. Buy low, sell high, and come out ahead on both sides. In reality, that's a fantasy. The market doesn't cooperate like that. It moves, shifts, and reacts to forces no individual can consistently predict. Trying to time it is like aiming at a moving target. You might get lucky once, but it's not a strategy.

The housing market will always fluctuate. Some periods favor buyers, others favor sellers, and occasionally you'll get a brief window where conditions feel balanced. But those windows are unpredictable and short-lived.

What actually matters is your timing—not the market's.

The right time to buy or sell is when it aligns with your life and your finances. If moving in the spring makes sense for you, do it. If winter works better, do that instead. Personal timing will outperform market timing every single time.

HOW SMALL NEGOTIATIONS COMPOUND OVER TIME

Small negotiation wins don't feel like much in the moment. But that's exactly why most people ignore them. That's a mistake.

A $2,000 price reduction. A seller credit for repairs. Getting closing costs covered. Slightly better terms on inspection or appraisal. Individually, these look minor. But stack them over multiple transactions, or even within a single deal, and they start to compound in a very real way.

Think about this.

Every dollar you don't spend upfront lowers your total cost basis. That means less cash out of pocket, lower risk, and often a better return when you sell the property. If you're buying and selling multiple times over your life, consistently squeezing out even small advantages can mean tens of thousands of dollars kept in your pocket instead of giving it away.

This can also compound psychologically. When you expect to negotiate, and do it well, you stop overpaying out of urgency or emotion. That discipline carries forward into every deal you touch.

And there's leverage compounding too. A better purchase price today gives you more flexibility tomorrow. Whether that's pricing aggressively when you sell, refinancing, or reinvesting into your next property.

Most people lose money in real estate not because of one big mistake, but because they repeatedly leave small amounts on the table. The edge isn't in one home run negotiation, it's in consistently winning the little battles.

Celebrate the small wins.

1.4 Loan Strategy From Day One

Most home buyers walk into a mortgage and just accept whatever structure they are given. That's an expensive mistake. If you don't set a strategy on day one, you end up reacting later instead of controlling the outcome.

Here's how to approach it like someone who actually understands money:

1. Start with the end in mind

Before you even pick a loan, decide what you want this house to do for you.

- Short-term hold (3-7 years)? Flexibility matters more than payoff speed.
- Long-term hold? Now interest savings and equity

build actually matter.

If you don't define this upfront, you'll pick the wrong loan for your situation.

2. Protect your cash flow first
Cash flow is oxygen. Once it's tight, everything else becomes a problem. That's why a 30-year fixed mortgage is often the smarter starting point, not because it's a cheaper payment overall, but because it gives you room to maneuver. You can always pay more. You can't pay less.

3. Control the rate, don't gamble on it.

- Lock a rate you can live with
- Don't bank on refinancing it later to save you
- If rates drop, great. You refinance from a position of strength
- If they don't, you're still fine

Too many people build their plan on a future that may never show up.

4. Use principal prepayments strategically
This is where most people leave money on the table.

If you go 30-year:

- Add consistent extra toward principal (even a few hundred a month matters)
- Or make 1 extra payment a year
- Target early years. This is where interest is heaviest

You essentially turn a 30-year into a 20 or even 15 without locking yourself into the higher payment.

5. Keep liquidity over obsession with payoff
Being house-rich and cash-poor is a trap.

Paying down your mortgage feels safe, but having accessible cash:

- Covers emergencies.
- Creates investment opportunities.
- Prevents you from taking on bad debt.

Don't drain your reserves just to knock down a low-interest loan faster.

6. Reevaluate every 2-3 years
Your loan strategy shouldn't be static.

- Income changes
- Rates change
- Life changes

Check if refinancing, recasting, or increasing payments makes sense. Most people "set it and forget it", and that's how they overpay.

The smartest move for most people is a 30-year fixed rate mortgage with intentional overpayment. Opposed to a 15-year loan that boxes you in. How you use the loan is strategy.

15 VS 30 YEAR (REAL WEALTH IMPACT)

I get asked this question often. What's the difference between a 30-year fixed rate mortgage and a 15-year fixed rate mortgage, and which one is best? Most people treat this like a simple "which is better" question. Unfortunately it's not that simple. It's a trade-off, and if you don't understand the trade-offs, you'll choose the wrong option.

Let's take a look at a 30-year fixed rate mortgage:

- Lower monthly payment
- More flexibility with your cash flow
- Higher interest rate (typically)
- Way more interest paid over time

This is the "breathing room" option. It keeps your payment manageable and gives you margin for life. Things like investing, emergencies, and opportunities. The downside? You pay for that flexibility with interest.

Let's explore a 15-year fixed rate mortgage:

- Higher monthly payments
- Lower interest rate
- Massive interest savings over the life of the loan
- Builds equity much faster

The real difference that most people miss. It's not about interest rate, it's about cash flow vs control.

- If you go with a 15-year, the bank is forcing you to be disciplined

- If you go with a 30-year, *you* have to be disciplined

A lot of people think they'll invest the difference with a 30-year, and then don't. That's where the 15-year quietly wins.

Here's a smarter way to think about it:
- If the 15-year payment stretches you even a little, it's risky. One income hiccup and you're stressed.
- If you're disciplined and want flexibility, go with the 30-year, but pay extra toward principle like a 15-year when it makes sense for you.

The best loan isn't the one with the lowest rate. It's the one you can live with consistently without putting yourself in a corner.

INTEREST RATES VS FLEXIBILITY

Most home buyers lean the wrong way because they chase the lowest rate without thinking about flexibility. It's about certainty vs. control.

Here's the breakdown:

Lower Interest Rate = Less Flexibility

Think 30-year fixed, traditional loans.

Some pro's:
- Predictable payment forever
- Protection if rates rise
- Easier to budget long-term

Some cons:

- Higher total interest over time
- Slower equity buildup
- Less adaptable if your life changes

Most people lock into a 30-year, then move or refinance within 5-10 years anyway.

More Flexibility = Often Higher or Variable Rates
Think Adjustable Rate Mortgages, or creative strategies.

Some examples:

- Adjustable Rate Mortgage (ARM)
- Paying extra toward principal
- Temporary rate buydowns

Some pros:

- Lower initial payments (ARMs)
- Faster equity
- Ability to adapt to future plans

Some cons:

- Payment uncertainty (ARMs)
- Higher monthly obligation
- Requires discipline

Flexibility only works if you actually use it strategically. Otherwise it introduces risk. It's not about what rate is best? It's how long will you realistically hold this loan.

Consider this:
If you're staying in the home 10-15 years:

- Fixed rate = safer, more predictable

If you're staying 3-7 years:

- Flexibility wins (ARM, lower upfront cost, etc.)

If you're aggressive financially:

- Flexibility + extra payments = you beat the system

Don't pick a loan. Pick a plan. Use a structure that gives you options, not just comfort. Build in the ability to pay extra without penalty. Keep cash flow strong so you're not trapped.

PMI, DOWN PAYMENT STRATEGY, AND OPPORTUNITY COST

PMI (Private Mortgage Insurance) kicks in when you put less than 20% down on a home.

The typical cost is:

- 0.3% to 1.5% of the loan amount annually

For example:
$400k home, 10% down = $150-300 a month PMI

It's important to know that PMI is temporary, dropping off around 20% equity, with the option to accelerate the removal with appreciation or extra payments.

Let's talk Down Payment Strategy.

Most people think they need 20% down to buy a home.

That's outdated thinking.

Here are two different strategies:

A. "Safe" Approach (20% down)
- No PMI
- Lower monthly payment
- Less risk psychologically

B. "Strategic" Approach (5-15% down)
- Pay PMI
- Keep more cash
- By sooner
- Preserve liquidity

The second approach is often financially superior, if you use the freed-up cash intelligently.

Next, let's talk opportunity cost. This is where the real decision is made.

Every extra dollar you put into your house is a dollar that:
- Isn't invested elsewhere
- Isn't used for business growth
- Isn't kept as liquidity for other opportunities

For example:
You have $80,000:
Option 1: Put it all into the house (20% down)
Option 2: Put $40,000 down, keep $40,000

Ask yourself:
Can that $40,000 earn more than the cost of PMI + interest difference?

If yes, lower down payment wins.
If no, higher down payment wins.

Let's simplify this thought:
PMI cost = $2,500 year
$40,000 at 7% = $2,800 a year

You're already ahead and still liquid!

People tend to avoid PMI because it seems wasteful. But they'll happily lock $80,000 into a house earning 3-5% appreciation annually. That's not logical, that's emotional.

So when should you put 20% down?

- You're cash-poor monthly and need lower payments
- You're risk-averse and sleep matters more than optimization
- You have no better use for the money
- Rates are high and guaranteed "return" from debt reduction is attractive

When looking at PMI, your down payment strategy, and opportunity cost, it's best to do what's right for your individual situation. It may even help to seek the expertise of a financial planner to get a better idea.

SECTION 2
UNDERSTANDING HOME EQUITY

2.1 What Home Equity Is And How It Works Definition

The equity in your home can be a powerful financial tool when used properly. Home equity is the portion of your home that you truly own. It's the difference between your home's market value and what you still owe on your mortgage. Equity can be a powerful tool that can better your financial situation and increase your wealth and net worth.

For example: If your home is worth $350,000, and you owe $200,000, your home equity is $150,000.

The amount of equity you have fluctuates depending on what the housing market does-which I will explain later in this section.

HOW EQUITY GROWS

Here are some common ways home equity grows:

1. Paying down your mortgage

Each payment reduces your loan balance.

2. Home value rising

If the market increases and your home appreciates, your equity grows.

3. Making home improvements

Upgrades that add value can boost equity. So why does it matter if equity grows or not?

The growth of home equity matters when you need to borrow against it in the form of a home equity loan, or HELOC (Home Equity Line of Credit). A home equity loan is an installment loan that gives you a lump sum of cash upfront for whatever you need money for. A HELOC is a home equity line of credit that works the same way as a credit card, where you only use what you need. Both loans have their benefits.

There are benefits that occur when equity grows. Equity growth can increase your net worth, can help you you move up to your next home in the form of a down payment, and even pay off higher rate credit cards.

Typically the interest rate on a home equity loan is less when compared to other types of loans. This makes it a more attractive option.

THE ROLE OF MARKET APPRECIATION

The equity in your home is tied closely to what the health of the housing market is and what it does on a daily basis. If the housing market is showing signs of growth, the equity in your home will grow. If the market is showing signs of decline, your equity will decrease. As a homeowner, you should expect the market to fluctuate back and forth on a regular basis. More often than not, homes appreciate year after year, with some years being better than others.

2.2 How To Calculate Your Home's Equity-Simple Formula

When looking to calculate your home's equity, there is a simple formula I like to use. While we touched on this earlier in this section, I feel it's worth repeating for clarification. To properly calculate equity, we must know two numbers, the homes current market value, and your remaining mortgage balance.

TOOLS AND METHODS TO ESTIMATE CURRENT VALUE

There are multiple ways to get the valuation of your home. You can get your home's market value by hiring a home appraiser, requesting a comparative market analysis from a realtor®, or looking at online estimates of homes that have sold in your area (not as accurate). Whatever method you choose, always remember that your value is a snapshot in time, and can fluctuate often. This is because homes are bought and sold daily.

Now that you know how to get your home's value, it's

time to look at your mortgage statement to get an idea of what you owe. This step is pretty simple. Now that we have these two numbers, it's time to apply the formula.

The formula is as follows:

Home Equity = Current Market Value - Remaining Mortgage Balance

Whatever number you come up with is the amount of equity you have in your home.

Now that you have a better understanding of how to calculate equity, it's time to consider what the percentage of equity is that you have in your home. Oftentimes lenders will calculate the percentage of equity you have when you are considering getting a loan with your home as collateral. This is referred to as LTV (Loan-To-Value). If your home is worth $350,000 and your mortgage balance is $140,000, your equity is at 40%.

When we look at the guidelines of what lenders will lend up to, many will lend up to 80%, while others may lend more. This means you can pull equity out of your home in the form of a loan up to 80% of what your home is worth. It's important to know what the lender will go up to when considering a home equity loan.

Here's the formula for calculating Loan To Value:

Current LOAN BALANCE divided by your HOME VALUE x 100 = LOAN TO VALUE

WHEN TO GET A PROFESSIONAL VALUATION

So how do you know when it's time to get a professional valuation on your home? I can tell you this decision should not be made because you are just 'curious' about the value.

A valuation should be considered:

Before you list your home

When considering selling your home, never rely on home websites that give an 'estimate' without looking at your home. Second, make sure you are within 3 months before selling to get an accurate valuation.

Major equity move

If you feel your home has increased in value enough to remove PMI (Private Mortgage Insurance), then it may be time to get a valuation, typically from an appraiser in this case. PMI is insurance that protects the lender, not the homeowner, if a borrower stops making payments on their mortgage. It's typically required when a buyer puts less than 20% down on a conventional home loan.

After significant improvements

If you've added square footage to your home, finished

the basement, upgraded major systems, and renovated rooms, it may be time to get your home reassessed.

Divorce or estate planning

When going through divorce or setting up an estate, it's important to have concrete numbers for the professional.

Property Tax Appeal

If you feel your property taxes are inflated, a professional valuation can give some clarity.

Market Shift

If your financial strategy depends on current value, it's time to get a valuation that is based on current homes in the area.

If you're not making a financial move, you probably don't need a valuation. If your value affects legal matters, lending, or large sums of money, a valuation can be helpful. Most of these things I just shared can be done by reaching out to a home appraiser. Although if you are considering selling the home, a real estate professional is the way to go.

SECTION 3 SMART REFINANCING STRATEGIES

3.1 What Is Refinancing and When Does It Make Sense?

In the last section I shared with you how you can use your home equity to pay off other high interest debt or fund home improvement projects. Now we will dive into what refinancing is and when it makes sense to do so.

Refinancing is the process of replacing your current mortgage with a new loan, usually to get better terms or access the equity in your home.

There are different types of refinancing options:

Cash-Out Refinance

When you refinance to get equity out, it's known as a refinance cash-out. You can change your mortgage terms and get cash back at closing. This is a popular option because you can get the equity out of your home at a lower interest rate than that of a standard home equity loan or HELOC.

Rate-And-Term Refinance
If you were to just refinance your mortgage without tapping into your home's equity, that would be referred to as a rate-and-term refinance. An example of a rate -and-term refinance is when you go from a mortgage of $150,000 at a 6% interest rate, to a rate of, let's say 4%, without changing your loan amount.

So, why do people refinance their mortgage?

WHEN TO REFINANCE
People refinance their mortgage for multiple reasons.

Here are some reasons why:

1. Lower the interest rate
It can be advantageous to refinance a mortgage to get a better rate, thus a lower monthly payment. It just has to make sense once you calculate closing costs into the refinance.

2. Reduce your monthly payment
Getting a better mortgage payment should always be top of mind, unless you have a small balance left to pay off.

3. Shorten the loan term
Many homeowners make the switch from a 30-year to a 15-year fixed-rate mortgage to save a ton of interest.

While this saves alot of interest, you must know that the payment will be higher, because of the shorter term.

4. Tap into the home equity

You just learned about the refinance cash-out option. This is a common reason why homeowners refinance. This is a great way to get access to cash for whatever you need it for.

5. Switch the loan type

Sometimes homeowners will change the loan type they have, oftentimes from an FHA loan to a standard 30-year fixed, because the monthly cost is less. There could be various other reasons why this would happen.

WHEN NOT TO REFINANCE

We just explored why many people consider refinancing their mortgage. Now let's explore when it's not the right time to refinance:

1. The closing costs outweigh the savings.

If your closing costs are high and it doesn't make sense to do the refinance, then don't. Always ask what the costs are to refinance.

2. You're planning to sell soon.

If you're looking to sell your home soon, it might not make sense to refinance. I can only think of one time when it makes sense to refinance before selling, and that's if you are pulling out a small portion of your equity to make an improvement that would add value to your home, and get you a higher offer price.

3. Your interest rate won't improve much.
If the proposed rate is not much lower than what you currently have, it might not make sense to refinance. Unless you are pulling out cash from your equity.

4. You already have a low interest rate.
If you are one of the lucky ones who, in recent years, obtained a lower interest rate, then it probably doesn't make sense to change it.

5. You'll reset your loan term.
When you refinance a mortgage, you reset your loan term. An example of this is if you refinance a mortgage where you have 20 years left, but you refinance to a 30-year term. By doing this you will accrue so much more interest.

6. Your credit score has dropped.
If you obtained a mortgage when your credit scores were high, but now your credit is less than stellar, it could cost you more to refinance, because of the higher rate. The worse your credit is, the higher the interest rate.

7. You'd lose certain loan benefits.
If your current mortgage is a government-backed loan and you refinance into a conventional loan, you may lose benefits unique to those programs such as a loss of the no/low down payment feature, you may have

to pay PMI (private mortgage insurance) if you don't have 20% equity, a loss of the eligibility of a streamline process which requires less paperwork, an appraisal waiver, and a simplified qualification process.

8. You're taking cash-out and reducing your equity.
While it can be beneficial in many cases to pull from your home's equity, there's a con to doing so. When you pull out equity, you reduce the amount that is available from your home. You also run the risk of being underwater, meaning owing more than the home is worth, should the housing market show signs of weakness.

9. Prepayment penalties on your current mortgage.
Sometimes lenders apply prepayment penalties to a mortgage if you pay it off, either with cash or through a refinance. It's important to find out if there is a prepayment penalty on your current mortgage.

10. Your Debt-To-Income ratio is high.
First, debt-to-income ratio is a measure lenders use to see how much of your monthly income goes towards paying debts.

Here is the formula:

DEBT TO INCOME = (Total monthly debt payments / Gross Monthly Income) x 100

Example: Total monthly debt payments: $1,800
Gross Monthly Income: $6,000

DEBT TO INCOME = (1,800 / 6,000) x 100 = 30%

Lenders like to see applicants at a DTI of 36% or lower. With a DTI of 50% being considered high risk.

Not every particular situation calls for a refinance. Sometimes it doesn't make sense to refinance a current mortgage, because you have such a great interest rate. I am a firm believer, that in many cases, refinancing is a great option.

3.2 How Refinancing Can Build Wealth

Refinancing can be a great tool to build wealth. When done right, it can improve your current financial situation, fund value improving projects, and reduce the amount of interest you pay on loans.

LOWERING MONTHLY PAYMENTS TO SAVE OVER TIME

Refinancing can lower your monthly payment, allowing you to apply the savings to other debt or pay more towards principal on your mortgage. You can also increase your monthly cash flow by lowering your payment.

SHORTENING LOAN TERMS TO BUILD EQUITY FASTER

Shortening your mortgage term, say from a 30-year loan to a 15-year loan term, can build equity faster, because more of your monthly payment goes toward principal rather than interest.

Here's a step by step breakdown:

1. How mortgage payments are divided

Every mortgage payment is split into:

- **Principal** - the portion that reduces your loan balance
- **Interest** - the portion paid to the lender
- **Taxes** - property taxes escrowed monthly
- **Insurance** - homeowners and/or mortgage insurance

With a longer-term loan (like 30 years), early payments are mostly interest. With a shorter-term loan (like 15 years), interest accrues less because the principal is paid down faster.

2. Faster principal reduction

Example; $300,000 loan at 6%.

- **30-year term:** First-year payments are roughly 21% principal, 79% interest.
- **15-year term:** First-year payments are roughly 45% principal, 55% interest.

3. Less interest paid overall

Shorter-term loans have higher monthly payments, but total interest paid over the life of the loan is much lower. This means more of your money goes into owning the home, rather than paying the lender.

4. Equity growth example

If your home is worth $350,000 and you owe $300,000:

- With a 30-year loan, you might build $30,000 of equity in the first 5 years.

- With a 15-year loan, you might build $60,000+ of equity in the same period—roughly double.

Shortening the term increases monthly payments, but accelerates equity growth and saves interest, effectively letting you own your home outright sooner.

USING CASH-OUT REFINANCING FOR VALUE ADDING IMPROVEMENTS

Pulling cash from your home's equity can be a great way to fund home improvement projects that add value to your home. At the time of this writing, the average fixed mortgage rate is around 6%. Where else can you borrow money at such a low rate! We will talk more about this in the next section.

3.3 Avoiding Refinance Mistakes

It's important to avoid mistakes however you can when considering a refinance. From choosing the right lender, to knowing what the cost of the loan is, making a sound decision starts with the proper research. The good thing is, you have this book! Some of the things you should avoid are lenders who take too long to implement the process, promotional rates that increase after you sign, and high closing costs.

UNDERSTANDING CLOSING COSTS

Understanding closing costs is the first step in deciding which lender to choose for your refinance.

Some important questions you should ask a lender are:

- How much are their costs?
- Are there any hidden fees?
- Is the rate a promotional rate?
- Is the lender reputable?

By asking these questions, you are determining if the lender is right for you.

AVOIDING FREQUENT REFINANCES

Refinancing your mortgage multiple times can seem like a way to save money or lower your payments, but there are several reasons why it's often best to avoid doing it too frequently:

1. Closing costs add up

Refinancing multiple times can be expensive. It can end up costing you more than what you are saving when you often change your loan. Look at what the break even point is and decide from there.

2. Resetting the loan term

We went over this in the last section. Resetting your loan term from a shorter term to a longer term is a very expensive maneuver and should be avoided if possible.

3. Impact on equity

When you refinance to access equity, you reduce what equity you have available to you. Not to mention you increase your chances of owing more than the home is worth.

4. Possible higher interest costs

Just like resetting your loan can cost you thousands more in interest, refinancing can add interest to your mortgage balance.

5. Credit score affects

Every time you have your credit pulled, it affects your scores slightly. While there are what's called "soft pulls", at the end of the day, it impacts your credit. Especially if you are adding debt to your credit report. When comparing lenders, do it in a short period of time.

6. Complexity and stress

Refinancing can be a somewhat stressful process. You have to provide income documentation, go through each step of the process, and wait patiently as the lender works on your loan. This can be stressful for many people.

WHY COMPARING MULTIPLE LENDERS MATTERS

One of the best pieces of advice I give clients, and homeowners alike, is that you should always compare 2-3 lenders when considering a refinance. Even if you get a referral from a reliable source, still make sure to see what other lenders are offering.

Some questions you should ask are:

- What are your closing costs?
- What is your interest rate without paying points?
- How long have you been writing loans?
- What is your turn around time to complete the process?

Asking the right questions will put you in a much better position of moving forward with the right lender for you.

SECTION 4 HOME IMPROVEMENTS THAT ACTUALLY ADD VALUE

4.1 High-ROI (Return On Investment) Renovations

High-return ROI home improvements are upgrades that tend to increase a home's value more than they cost by improving functionality, efficiency, and buyer appeal. The following are home improvements that actually add value to a home.

KITCHENS AND BATHROOMS

Updating kitchens and bathrooms often adds value, because these spaces have the biggest impact on how buyers perceive a home. I can tell you that when I show homes, these are the first rooms a buyer gravitates towards.

Let's explore the top reasons why buyers focus on these areas:

1. High buyer priority

Kitchens and bathrooms are the most used and emotionally driven rooms in a home. Buyers often decide how they feel about a property within minutes, and outdated kitchens or baths can make a home feel older-even if everything else is in good shape.

2. Strong return on investment

While you may not recoup 100% of renovation costs, kitchen and bathroom updates consistently rank among the top improvements for resale value. Minor upgrades including new countertops, refreshed cabinets, modern fixtures, or updated lighting can deliver an especially strong return.

3. Improved functionality

Modern layouts, better storage, and energy-efficient appliances or fixtures make these rooms more practical. Homes that function well are easier to sell and often command higher prices, because buyers see less work ahead.

4. Move-in ready appeal

Many buyers prefer move-in ready homes that don't require a ton of work. Updated kitchens and baths reduce "to-do lists", helping a home sell faster and potentially attract multiple offers.

5. Perception of overall condition

Updated kitchens and baths signal that a home has been well maintained. Buyers often assume that if these big-ticket areas are updated, the rest of the home has been cared for too.

6. Competitive edge in the market

In competitive markets, updated kitchens and baths can be the deciding factor between two similar homes, often justifying a higher sales price.

Strategic kitchen and bathroom upgrades don't just-improve aesthetics, they enhance functionality, buyer confidence, and overall marketability, making them some of the smartest investments a homeowner can make before selling.

CURB APPEAL UPGRADES

Curb appeal upgrades don't have to be expensive to make a big impact. Matter of fact, most can be done in a weekend.

Here are some of the most effective ways homeowners can boost their home's first impression, and often it's value:

1. Landscaping refresh

- Trim overgrown shrubs and trees
- Add fresh mulch to garden beds
- Plant seasonal flowers - low-maintenance perennials
- Keep the lawn mowed and edged

2. Front door upgrade

- Paint or stain the front door in a welcoming, modern color
- Replace worn hardware (handle, lock, knocker)
- Add a decorative wreath or seasonal accent

3. Exterior paint touch-ups

- Touch up peeling or faded paint on siding, trim, or shutters
- Repaint shutters or window trim for contrast

4. Outdoor lighting

- Update porch lights with modern fixtures
- Add pathway or solar lights for evening curb appeal
- Ensure all bulbs work and provide warm, inviting light

5. Driveway and walkways

- Power wash concrete, brick, or pavers
- Repair cracks or uneven sections
- Define walkways with edging or plants

6. House numbers and mailbox

- Install modern, easy-to-read house numbers
- Replace or repaint the mailbox
- Coordinate finishes (black, bronze, brushed nickel)

7. Roof and gutters

- Clean gutters and downspouts
- Remove debris or moss from the roof
- Make minor repairs where needed

8. Windows and screens

- Clean windows inside and out
- Repair or replace screens
- Add simple window boxes for charm

9. Add potted plants or planters

- Update outdoor furniture or a welcome mat
- Paint or stain railings and steps

10. Garage door update

- Paint the garage door or upgrade hardware
- Replace an outdated door if budget allows

Curb appeal sets expectations before a buyer steps inside. A clean, well-maintained exterior suggests the home has been cared for, often leading to higher offers and quicker sales. Remember, the better the curb appeal, the better the offer price.

FLOORING, PAINT, AND LIGHTING IMPROVEMENTS

You'll be amazed at what new flooring, a fresh coat of paint, and minor updates to lighting can do to a property.

Let's explore what each of these areas can do to a home:

New flooring: Foundation of a first impression

- **Instant Modernization:** Replacing worn carpet or dated vinyl with hardwood (number one choice for resale) luxury vinyl plank, or updated tile immediately refreshes the space.
- **Perceived cleanliness and care:** Buyers often equate new floors with a well-maintained home.
- **Flow and cohesion:** Using consistent flooring throughout the main living areas makes the home feel larger and more cohesive.
- **Strong ROI:** Flooring upgrades frequently return a

high-percentage of their cost, especially in living rooms, kitchens and hallways.

Fresh paint: The biggest visual upgrade for the cost

- **Brightens and enlarges spaces:** Light, neutral colors make rooms feel bigger and more inviting.
- **Modernizes a space instantly:** Painting over bold or outdated colors helps a home appeal to more buyers.
- **Highlights features of the home:** Fresh paint makes trim, cabinets, and architectural items stand out.
- **Low cost-high payoff:** Paint is one of the most least expensive upgrades with one of the biggest impacts on buyers perception.

Updated lighting fixtures: Set's the mood

- **Improves ambiance:** Modern fixtures create warmth and comfort while eliminating dark or shadowy areas.
- **Style statement:** Lighting is often viewed as a design feature-dated fixtures can age an entire home.
- **Energy efficiency:** New LED fixtures lower energy costs and attract eco-conscious buyers.
- **Functionality:** Better lighting improves usability in kitchens, bathrooms and workspaces.

When done together, new flooring, new paint, and updated light fixtures:

- Make the home feel move-in ready
- Increase perceived value
- Reduce buyer objections

- Often help a home sell faster and for more money.

4.2 Cost-Efficient Improvements

ENERGY-EFFICIENT UPDATES (INSULATION, WINDOWS, APPLIANCES)

Energy-efficient updates are a smart way for homeowners to lower utility costs, improve comfort, and increase resale appeal. Here are some of the most impactful upgrades, ranging from simple fixes to bigger investments:

LOW COST/HIGH IMPACT UPDATES

- **LED lighting throughout the home:** Uses up to 75% less energy than incandescant bulbs and lasts years longer.
- **Smart power strips:** Reduce "phantom" energy use from tv's, computers, and enteratinment systems.
- **Programmable or smart thermostats:** Automatically adjust temperatures when the home is empty or at night.
- **Weatherstripping and caulking:** Seals air leaks around doors, windows, and attics to reduce heating and cooling loss.

INSULATION AND AIR QUALITY IMPROVEMENTS

- **Attic and insulation upgrades:** One of the best returns on investment for energy efficiency.
- **Sealing ductwork:** Prevents conditioned air from escaping into attics or crawl spaces.
- **Energy-efficient ceiling fans:** Improve air circulation and reduce HVAC workload.

WINDOW AND DOOR ENHANCEMENTS

- **Energy-efficient windows (Double or triple pane):** Reduce heat transfer and outside noise.
- **Insulated exterior doors:** Minimize drafts and improve temperature consistency.
- **Window treatments:** Help regulate indoor temperature year-round.

HVAC AND WATER HEATING UPGRADES

- **High-effiency HVAC systems:** Modern systems use less energy while improving indoor comfort.
- **Regular HVAC maintenance:** Keeps systems running efficiently and extends lifespan.
- **Tankless or high-efficiency water heaters:** Reduce energy waste by heating water on demand.
- **Low-flow showerheads and faucets:** Save both water and energy used to heat it.

RENEWABLE AND SMART HOME OPTIONS

- **Solar panels:** Lower long-term energy costs and increase home value in many markets.
- **Energy-efficient appliances (ENERGY STAR®):** Reduce electricity and water usage.
- **Smart lighting systems:** Allow homeowners to automate and control lighting remotely.

Why these updates matter.

Energy-efficient upgrades:

- Lower monthly utility bills.
- Improve indoor comfort year-round.

- Appeal to eco-conscious buyers.
- Often qualify for tax credits or utility rebates.
- Help homes sell faster and with fewer buyer objections.

Please refer to the end of this book for seasonal checklists as reference.

4.3 Projects That Rarely Add Value

This is a topic that catches many homeowners by surprise. While some projects feel like "upgrades", they often don't translate into higher resale value.

Here are some common home projects that rarely add value and sometimes even work against you at resale:

OVER-CUSTOMIZATION

Believe it or not, there is a such thing as overdoing it on a home project. These can include custom murals, bold wallpaper, highly specific design features, built-in's tailored to a hobby i.e. wine room, music studio, or home gyms that replace bedrooms. These "upgrades" can cause a negative effect at resale. Other home projects that negatively affect resale are luxury upgrades that exceed the neighborhood such as high-end appliances, and spa-level bathrooms in modest homes. Any type of home project that exceeds what your neighbors are doing should be avoided.

POOLS IN CERTAIN MARKETS

Pools are expensive to install and maintain. Many buyers see them as a liability, rather than a bonus. In cold climates especially, pools rarely return their cost. Some of the biggest turn offs are inground pools, because they are very expensive to remove from a yard. Sometimes though, a luxurious pool in the yard of a high-end home can be attractive to buyers.

CONVERTING BEDROOMS INTO SPECIALTY ROOMS

Turning a bedroom into an office, closet, or media room, and/or removing a bedroom to enlarge a living space can have a negative effect on resale. Bedroom count has a huge effect on resale value.

GARAGE CONVERSIONS

While it may be great to have additional living space, converting a garage into a living space or storage is a major turnoff to buyers. After all, where will they park?

DIY PROJECTS WITHOUT PROFESSIONAL QUALITY

DIY projects such as poorly installed flooring, tile or cabinetry, visible shortcuts in the work and non-permitted work are red flags to a buyer. Matter of fact, many of these issues come up during home inpsections and appraisals.

HIGH-END LANDSCAPING WITH HEAVY MAINTENANCE

Landscaping is a major area to keep an eye on when thinking about resale. Exotic plants, water features, or elaborate gardens can hinder a home buyers efforts to visualize maintaining it. Buyers appreciate curb appeal, but not ongoing upkeep costs.

SOLAR PANELS (SOMETIMES)

Generally, solar panels increase a home's value, with multiple studies showing that they can make homes sell faster, and for more money. Home buyers see solar panels as valuable upgrades, recognizing the long-term savings on electricity bills and energy independence. There is additional savings in areas that have higher utility rates.

It's important to note however, that leased solar panels can complicate a home sale because not all buyers want to assume a contract or have maintenance respponsibilities. It's best if they are owned and not leased.

4.4 How to Decide What to Improve

Deciding what to improve in your home starts with balancing livability, budget, and long-term value, especially if resale or wealth-building is part of your plan.

ANALYZING YOUR MARKET

It's important to know what your local housing market is doing, when considering selling, to determine whether or not you will get a return on your money.

For example, if you're looking to sell your home and the market favors home sellers, it may not be worth it to spend the time and money to make an upgrade, because buyers will still pay top dollar to win your listing. However, if the market favors home buyers, you will want to make upgrades to entice buyers towards your home.

Real estate is hyper-local. Narrow your focus to your specific city, neighborhood, or subdivision. Compare similar home types (square footage, amount of rooms, etc.). Also, look into local school ratings and zoning requirements. Study recent sales of homes that actually closed. Sold homes tell you what buyers are actually paying. Look at sales from the last 3-6 months. Focus on homes similar to yours. Note the sale price vs list price. Pay attention to the condition and upgrades.

It's not enough to look at what the closed homes sold for, you should also know what the current (active) homes on the market are listed for. Active listings show your competition right now. Note how many homes are currently for sale, what they are priced at, how long they have been on the market, and have they reduced their price recently.

When looking at how long a home has been on the market, you should know the following: (DOM is days on market)

Short DOM = Strong demand / sellers market
Long DOM = slower market / buyer leverage

Lastly, look at price trends. Are prices trending up, down, or flat? Compare year-over-year and quarter-over- quarter changes. Remember, consistency matters more than the news headlines.

Evaluating supply and demand is key to analyzing

the market. This can be broken down into how many months of inventory are available. Under 3 months of inventory means the market favors sellers. 4-6 months of inventory is a balanced market favoring both buyers and sellers. Anything 6 months or over means the market favors buyers.

Another factor to consider when analyzing the market are interest rates and buyer behavior. Mortgage rates directly impact affordability. Higher rates may reduce the buyer pool. Incentives, concessions, and price flexibility often increase when rates rise.

Seasonal patterns also play a factor in analyzing the market. Spring and early Summer are typically more active. Whereas Fall and Winter can mean less competition but more serious buyers.

Many times the news headlines share doom and gloom, especially when it comes to the housing market. The national news doesn't always reflect your local market. One neighborhood can have hot activity while another doesn't. Lastly, use market data to make strategic decisions.

There are important questions to ask before making an important decision. They are:

- Is now the right time to sell?
- What upgrades will actually matter in this market?
- How should pricing strategy change based on conditions?

A strong market analysis focuses on local data, comparable homes, and current buyer behavior-not guesswork or headlines.

WORKING WITH A REAL ESTATE PROFESSIONAL

If there is one piece of advice you should take from this section, it's that there is a difference between a real estate agent and a realtor®. Many real estate agents use the term "realtor®" loosely. In reality, a realtor® is a higher degree of real estate agent. Like a real estate agent with a masters degree. A realtor® is a member of the National Association of Realtors® (NAR) and follows a lengthy code of ethics to ensure they represent their clients the best way possible.

Choosing the right real estate professional can make the process of selling a home less stressful, with proper communication and expertise guiding you through each step.

So why does this matter to you?

It's crucial to not only choose a realtor®, but one that is capable of giving you the best analysis of your local market and how it affects your property. One way to identify a true realtor® is to simply ask if they are one. And never settle for a family member or friend who is new to the business. Buying and selling a home is by far the biggest decision you can make, and you don't want to leave this to chance.

BUDGETING AND PLANNING TIPS

Here are practical, easy-to-apply tips for budgeting and planning written to work for everyday life and long-term goals, especially helpful if you're thinking in terms of financial stability and wealth building.

1. Start with clear goals

Before you budget, know why you're budgeting. If you're budgeting for the short-term, think monthly bills, emergency fund, and upcoming repairs. If you're budgeting for the mid-term, think home upgrades, paying down debt, and saving for a move. For the long-term, think retirement, investment properties, and creating financial freedom. Always assign a purpose to your budgeting. It makes budgeting easier to stick to.

2. Know your true monthly numbers

Many fail at budgeting because expenses are underestimated. To combat this, try fixed costs (mortgage/rent, insurance, utilities), variable costs (food, gas, entertainment) and don't forget irregular expenses (home repairs, car maintenance, holidays). It also helps to look at your last 3-6 months bank statements for accuracy.

3. Use a simple budget framework

Choose a structure you can realistically maintain:

Use the 50/30/20 Rule

- 50% needs
- 30% wants
- 20% savings and debt reduction

Or Zero-Based Budget (every dollar has a job).

The best budget is the one you will actually follow.

4. Pay yourself first

- Treat savings like a bill.
- Automate transfers into savings or investment accounts.
- Build an emergency fund (3-6 months of expenses).
- Increase savings when income increases-not spending.

5. Plan for the "Non-monthly" costs

- These often derail budgets.
- Home maintenance (1-3% of home value annually).
- Insurance deductibles.
- Taxes and annual subscriptions.

Create a fund so that these expenses don't end up being a surprise.

6. Reduce before you restrict

Instead of cutting everything:

- Negotiate insurance costs.
- Review subscriptions quarterly.
- Shop around for services annually.

Small reductions can have a compounding effect over time.

7. Plan quarterly, not just monthly

- Life changes-your budget should too.
- Review income and expenses every 90 days.
- Adjust for seasonality (utilities, holidays, school costs).

- Revisit goals regularly.

8. Align spending with your values
If something matters to you, budget for it guilt-free. Cut spending that doesn't add value to your life.

9. Use tools-but keep it simple
- Spreadsheets
- Budgeting apps
- Dedicated checking account for bills

Complex systems lead to burnout. So keep it simple.

10. Budget with the future in mind
Every dollar should support where you're going, not just where you are. Ask yourself "Is this expense helping me build stability, freedom, or future opportunities?"

SECTION 5 LONG-TERM WEALTH BUILDING THROUGH HOMEOWNERSHIP

5.1 The Power of Time and Appreciation

When it comes to time and appreciation, I can personally say that a home can appreciate over time significantly. Every home my wife and I have owned has had a steady appreciation over the years. I can't think of any other investment that has an almost guaranteed appreciation as real estate.

One of the greatest advantages of owning a home is the power of time combined with appreciation. As years pass, real estate historically increases in value, allowing homeowners to build equity simply by owning their property. What I personally like about real estate is that it's easier to predict appreciation vs other investment vehicles such as stocks.

While markets can fluctuate in the short term, long-term homeownership has proven to be a reliable way to grow wealth. Each mortgage payment you make reduces your principal balance, and as the home appreciates, the owners equity grows. Over time, this steady combination can create significant financial security. This additional wealth can be used for opportunities too.

HOW HOME VALUES TREND UPWARD

As I mentioned in the last section, home values tend to trend upward over time. This is due to a combination of economic forces, housing fundamentals, and long-term demand.

Here are 7 things that better explain what I mean:

1. Inflation

As the cost of goods and services rises over time, so does the cost to build a home. Higher construction costs push prices upward, which supports higher home values overall.

2. Limited supply of land

Let's face it, there not making land anymore. Land is finite, especially in desirable areas. As population grows and available land becomes scarcer, demand increases, driving prices higher.

3. Population and household growth

More people and new households create ongoing demand for housing. Even during slower markets, people still need places to live, supporting long-term value growth.

4. Rising incomes over time
As wages increase over the long term, buyers can afford higher home prices, which naturally lifts market values.

5. Home improvements and maintenance
Many homeowners continually upgrade and maintain properties. These improvements raise individual values and elevate neighborhood prices as a whole.

Side note: One of the biggest mistakes I've seen home sellers make is trying to get top dollar for a property that has not been upgraded.

6. Desirable locations become more valuable
It's no secret that great neighborhoods command more money. Areas with good schools, job growth, amenities, and infrastructure improvements tend to see consistent appreciation over time.

7. Market cycles smooth out long-term
While housing markets experience ups and downs, history shows that declines are usually temporary. Over longer periods, values recover and continue to climb.

So, what's the bottom line?

Short-term fluctuations are normal, but over time, home values rise because housing is a limited, essential asset tied to population growth, inflation, and economic progress.

HISTORICAL APPRECIATION EXAMPLES

Historically, U.S. home values have appreciated about 3-4% per year on average over the long term. This roughly tracks inflation, but because homes are typically leveraged assets, the owner's equity growth is often much higher.

For example:
A $100,000 home appreciating at 3.5% annually:

- $141,000 after 10 years
- $200,000 after 20 years
- $280,000 after 30 years

Appreciation isn't always smooth, but time smooths volatility. Even with downturns, long-term ownership has historically reqarded patience.

Appreciation + mortgage paydown = powerful equity growth.

It's important to know that housing has outperformed many savings vehicles for average americans.

WHY PATIENCE IS KEY

When looking for a return on investment, owning a home is a long-term strategy. Real estate builds wealth over time, not overnight.

Here are the main reasons patience matters:

1. Appreciation Is Gradual, Not Instant

Home values typically increase slowly through market cycles. Short-term fluctuations happen, but long-term trends tend to move upward as demand, inflation, and population growth increase.

2. Time smooths out market ups and downs
Housing markets rise and fall. Homeowners who stay patient are more likely to ride out temporary downturns and benefit from recoveries rather than being forced to sell during a low point.

3. Equity grows even when prices are flat
This may seem hard to believe, but each mortgage payment reduces your loan balance. Over time, this "forced savings" builds equity regardless of short-term appreciation, rewarding homeowners who hold onto the property.

4. Inflation works in your favor
As inflation increases, replacement costs and home prices often rise, while your fixed mortgage payment stays the same. The longer you own, the more powerful this effect becomes.

5. Home improvements compound over time
Smart upgrades, neighborhood development, and infrastructure improvements don't pay off immediately, but their value becomes clearer over years of ownership.

6. Transaction costs favor long-term ownership
Buying and selling a home comes with siginficant costs.

Patience allows appreciation to outpace those expenses and create a true net gain.

So what's the bottom line?

Homeownership rewards consistency and time. Those who remain patient allow appreciation, equity growth, and market cycles to work together. This turns a home into a long-term wealth-building asset, rather than a short-term gamble.

5.2 Leveraging Your Equity Wisely

Leveraging your home equity wisely means using the value you've built in your home as a strategic tool, not an emotional or impulsive one.

When used thoughtfully, home equity can help fund renovations that increase value, consolidate high-interest debt, invest in additional real estate, or cover major life expenses at lower interest rates than many other loans. The key is ensuring the equity is working for you, not putting your home at an unnecessary risk.

Using equity wisely considers:

- The purpose of the funds.
- The return or long-term benefit.
- Your ability to comfortably manage payments.
- Market conditions and future gains.

Used responsibly, home equity can accelerate wealth-building. Used carelessly, it can erase years of progress. Your home equity is a powerful asset. Treat it like and investment tool and not a shortcut to cash.

HELOC'S FOR IMPROVEMENTS

HELOCS, or Home Equity Lines Of Credit, can be a smart way to upgrade your home. This is when used strategically. A HELOC allows you to borrow against the equity you've built, giving you flexible access to funds as needed rather than a lump sum. This makes it ideal for renovation projects that happen in stages.

Some of the reasons why homeowners use HELOC's are:

- Lower interest rates compared to credit cards or personal loans.
- Pay interest only on what you use.
- Flexible draw period for ongoing projects.
- Potential to increase home value with the right upgrades.

Smart ways to use a HELOC

- Kitchens, bathrooms, and energy-efficient upgrades.
- Necessary repairs that protect home value like replacing HVAC or a new roof.
- Projects that improve functionality and long-term appeal.
- Paying for an education.
- Covering emergency expenses.
- Paying a down payment on an investment property or investing in a small business.

Some important considerations:

- Borrow only for improvements that add value to the home.
- Have a clear budget and repayment plan.
- Remember your home is the collateral, so avoid overleveraging.

A HELOC can turn built-up equity into a more valuable home. Success, however, depends on choosing the right projects and borrowing responsibly. You would never want to borrow your home's equity to finance a vacation trip for example. That would not be wise.

FUNDING ADDITIONAL INVESTMENTS

Owning a home can be a great way to fund additional investments that can be beneficial to your financial situation. To get a better understanding of this, I put together a series of questions you should ask a financial planner before hiring them:

1. Are you a fiduciary at all times?

If they answer anything other than a clean, confident yes, run away. A fiduciary is legally required to put your interests first.

2. How are you paid?

- Ask how they are paid:
- Fee only (flat-fee or % of interest)?
- Commission-based?
- Hybrid?

3. What credentials do you hold-and why do they matter?
A serious planner should be able to explain the value of their credentials or designations.

- Certified Financial Planner Board of Standards (CFP)
- Chartered Financial Analyst Institute (CFA)

It's a red flag if they can't explain their designation.

4. Who is your typical client?
Do they mostly work with those in their thirties? Or do they focus on helping those in retirement? Specialization matters when it comes to finances.

5. What is your investment philosophy?
Ask these questions:

- Active trading?
- Long-term passive?
- Risk-managed?
- Insurance-heavy?

If they don't have a clear strategy, or if it sounds like hype, move on.

6. What services are included?
Do they provide:

- Tax planning?
- Retirement income modeling?
- Estate planning coordination?
- Risk analysis?
- Long-term care planning?

Or do they just manage a portfolio?

7. How will we measure success?

A sign of an amateur is when they say they 'beat the market'. You want to hear things like:

- Progress toward your financial goals
- Risk-adjusted returns
- Income sustainability
- Tax efficiency

8. Can you show me a sample financial plan?

If they hesitate, that's a problem.

9. What happens if something happens to you?

Is there a succession plan? A team? Or are you tied to one person?

10. Why should I hire you instead of managing this myself?

Make them sell their value. If they can't articulate what they do beyond 'invest your money', you don't need them.

USING HOME EQUITY FOR RETIREMENT STRATEGIES WITHOUT OVER-LEVERAGING

Home equity can play a meaningful role in retirement planning, but it must be approached with caution and intention. The goal is to support long-term security, not create new financial stress.

Here are some smart ways home equity can support retirement:

- Reducing high-interest debt before retirement to lower monthly obligations.
- Strategic downsizing to free up equity while cutting housing expenses.
- Funding necessary home modifications (aging in place upgrades).
- Supplementing cash-flow when coordinated with other retirement income sources.
- Real estate repositioning, such as selling and buying a more efficient or lower maintenance home.

To avoid over-leveraging, remember:

- Borrow only what you need, not the maximum available.
- Keep housing costs well within a fixed-income budget.
- Stress-test payments against future income reductions.
- Maintain an emergency reserve outside of home equity.
- Coordinate decisions with a financial advisor or tax professional.

Watch closely for these risks:

- Variable interest rates increasing payments.
- Reduced flexibility if markets or health circumstances change.
- Using equity for non-essential or depreciating expenses.

Home equity should act as a stability tool, not a substitute for income or savings. When used thoughtfully, alongside downsizing strategies, cash-flow planning, and professional guidance, equity can strengthen retirement without putting the home itself at risk.

5.3 Paying Off Your Mortgage Strategically

BIWEEKLY PAYMENTS

For many homeowners, a mortgage is the largest debt they will ever carry. Reducing interest costs and shortening the repayment period can dramatically improve financial freedom. One strategy that's gained popularity over recent decades is biweekly mortgage payments. This section explains what they are, how they work, and whether they make sense for you.

APPLYING EXTRA PRINCIPAL PAYMENTS

Before we can apply biweekly payments to our mortgage, we must understand what they are. Most mortgages are structured around monthly payments equalling 12 payments per year. A biweekly mortgage payment plan instead breaks the regular monthly payment in half and schedules payments every two weeks, rather than once per month.

There are 52 weeks in a year, which means 26 biweekly periods. Paying half a monthly payment every two weeks results in 13 full monthly payments over the year instead of 12. That extra payment helps reduce your principal balance faster, which accelerates your mortgage payoff and reduces interest costs. Some people may do better with a biweekly plan because the payments can seem more manageable.

WHY BIWEEKLY PAYMENTS SAVE MONEY

Here are some reasons why biweekly payments save money:

1. Extra principal reduces interest

Mortgage interest accrues daily on the outstanding balance. Paying down the principal sooner means less interest accrues over time. If you pay every two weeks instead of monthly, you're effectively reducing your balance throughout the year at a faster rate. That's compound interest working against the lender.

2. Shorter loan term

Without changing the payment size, biweekly payments reduce the effective life of the mortgage. On a 30-year mortgage, you might shave 3-6 years off the term. A shorter term means huge interest savings.

TWO WAYS TO SET UP BIWEEKLY PAYMENTS

1. Through your lender

Some lenders offer built-in biweekly plans:

- Automated
- May cost a fee
- Applies payments directly to principal.

Pros: Easy, set-and-forget

Cons: Fees or restrictions

2. DIY approach

You can simply make half-payments every two weeks directly:

- Write 26 half-payments each year.

- Ensure payments are applied to principal.

Pros: No fees, flexibility
Cons: Requires discipline

Confirm with your lender that your payments are being applied to your principal soon after you make the change. Don't wait until months end.

BENEFITS OF PAYING OFF EARLY VS. INVESTING ELSEWHERE

This is a great debate held by many people. Should you pay your home off early, or invest in other areas such as stocks, bonds, etc. Before we talk investments, let's explore the benefits of paying off a mortgage early:

1. Guaranteed, risk-free return

Paying extra towards your mortgage delivers a guaranteed return equal to your interest rate.

Example:

- 4% mortgage = guaranteed 4% return
- No market volatility
- No fees
- No taxes on the "return"

It's rare that you get this kind of certainty.

2. Massive interest savings

Interest compounds over decades. Paying early:

- Reduces total interest paid
- Shortens loan term by years
- Frees up future cash flow

On a 30-year loan, even small extra payments can save

tens or hundreds of thousands of dollars.

3. Increased monthly cash flow

Once the mortgage is paid off:

- No monthly payment
- Lower fixed expenses
- Easier retirement budgeting
- More flexibility during job changes or downturns

This is especially powerful for people nearing retirement.

4. Emotional and psychological benefits

This is often underestimated:

- Peace of mind
- Lower financial stress
- Feeling of ownership and stability
- Greater sense of security during economic uncertainty

You can't put a spreadsheet value on sleeping well at night.

5. Reduced risk in down markets

If the markets drop:

- Investments may lose value.
- Mortgage payments don't.

Owning your home outright reduces exposure to financial shocks. Now that we covered the benefits of paying your mortgage off early, let's explore the benefits of investing elsewhere.

1. Potentially higher returns

Historically:

- Stock markets average 7-10% long-term
- Mortgage rates are often 3-6%
- Investing can outperform paying off a low-rate mortgage, but returns are not guaranteed.

2. Liquidity and access to cash
Investments are:
- Easier to sell
- More Flexible
- Usable for emergencies or opportunities

Money locked into home equity is harder to access without refinancing or selling.

3. Tax advantages
Depending on the situation:
- Mortgage interest may be deductible
- Investment gains can be tax-advantaged (401k, IRA, Roth)

This varies widely by income and tax law.

Paying off a mortgage early is rarely the wrong decision. It's just not always the mathematically optimal one.

** The information provided is for educational and informational purposes only and should not be construed as tax, legal, or financial advice. I am not a licensed tax professional, financial advisor, or attorney. You should consult with qualified professionals regarding your specific situation before making any financial decisions.*

5.4 Transitioning To Your Next Property

Using equity as a down payment on your move-up home. Using the equity in your current home to put a sizeable down payment on your next home is highly achieveable and more common than you may think. By tapping into your equity, you can remove the need for mortgage insurance.

USING EQUITY AS A DOWN PAYMENT ON YOUR MOVE-UP HOME

Equity can be a great way to get you into your next home by applying it as a down payment.

Here are some methods to use equity for a move-up home:

- HELOC (Home Equity Line Of Credit)
- Bridge Loan
- Home Equity Loan
- Sale Proceeds

Now that we know the methods, let's dive into each one to get a better understanding.

HELOC (Home Equity Line Of Credit)

In the last section we covered the benefits of a HELOC for tapping into your home's equity. What you may not know is that using a HELOC can allow you to put a larger down payment on your next home, making it a safer investment.

Bridge Loan
Often called a 'swing loan', a bridge loan is a short-term, secured loan designed to 'bridge the gap' between the purchase of a new property and the sale of an existing one. These loans typically last 6-12 months, feature higher interest rates, and are repaid in a lump sum once the orginal home is sold.

Home Equity Loan
Similar to a HELOC, this type of loan provides a lump sum payment, which can be used to fund the down payment, usually allowing up to 80% of the home's equity to be borrowed.

Sale Proceeds
Selling the current home first provides the most straightforward method to use equity, and probably the most common. Though you may need temporary housing.

Leveraging your home's equity can make a home buyer more competitive and reduce monthly payments on the new, larger home.

DOWNSIZING FOR PROFIT

Downsizing a home for profit means selling a larger or higher-maintenanced home and moving into a smaller, more efficient property in a way that preserves and maximizes your home equity.

It's not simply about moving to a smaller space. It's

about making a strategic financial move that improves cash flow, reduces expenses, and strengthens long-term financial security.

When done correctly, downsizing can free up cash, lower monthly costs, and reduce financial stress, while still supporting your lifestyle and future goals.

So where does the profit come from?

1. Captured home equity
Many longtime homeowners, especially those who've owned for 20-30 years, have a significant amount of equity.

When you sell:
- Your mortgage may be low or paid off.
- Appreciation over time creates a large gap between the value and debt.
- That equity can be repositioned, not just stored in a house.

The 'profit' is the portion of equity left after:
- Paying off the existing mortgage.
- Covering selling costs.
- Purchasing the next home or securing a rental.

What remains can be used for:
- Retirement income.
- Healthcare costs.
- Emergency savings.

- Travel or lifestyle upgrades.
- Helping children or grandchildren.

2. Lowered monthly expenses

A smaller home often means:

- Lower property taxes.
- Reduced utility bills.
- Lower insurance costs.
- Less maintenance and repair spending.

Even a modest reduction in monthly expenses can add up to tens of thousands of dollars over time, which effectively increases profit without relying on market growth.

3. Reduced maintenance = preserved wealth

Larger homes are nice, but cost more to maintain:

- Roofs, HVAC systems, landscaping, and repairs
- Time, energy, and unexpected expenses

Downsizing helps homeowners:

- Avoid large future repair bills.
- Preserve cash instead of reinvesting it into an aging property.
- Reduce physical and emotional stress.

Less money spent on upkeep means more money kept in your pocket.

Downsizing for profit is highly dependant on when the home is sold.

A well-timed sale can:

- Maximize market value.
- Reduce the need for major renovations.
- Minimize time on the market.
- Avoid selling during a downturn, or after deferred maintenance becomes urgent.

Waiting too long can:

- Increase repair costs.
- Limit housing options.
- Force rushed decisions.
- Reduce net proceeds.

Strategic timing protects profit. Choosing the right property for your next home is important.

Profit isn't only made on the sale, it's also protected on the purchase.

A profitable downsizing plan considers:

- Purchase price relative to net proceeds.
- Long-term affordability.
- Property taxes and HOA fees.
- Accessibility and aging-in-place potential.
- Future resale value.

Sometimes the most profitable move isn't the smallest home, but the most efficient and well-located one. Downsizing for profit is not a one size fits all situation.

Downsizing works best when aligned with:

- Retirement timeline.
- Health considerations
- Income sources.
- Lifestyle priorities.
- Family dynamics.

For some, profit means maximizing cash. For others, it means lowering monthly obligations. Both points are valid, and both are forms of profit. Downsizing a home for profit is about turning years of homeownership into financial flexibility.

When done intentionally, it can:

- Increase cash reserves.
- Lower monthly expenses.
- Reduce risk.
- Simplify life.
- Support long-term financial security.

It's not about giving something up. It's about making your home work for you in the next chapter of your life.

TURNING YOUR CURRENT HOME INTO A RENTAL

I have to admit, I'm not a fan of this option. But I would be providing a disservice to you if I didn't let you know this option exists.

Converting your home into a rental can be a smart way to build long-term wealth, create monthly income, and leverage your real estate investment. However, it's important to understand the responsibilities, costs, and legal requirements *before* making the move.

Here are 9 things you should know before renting your home:

1. Understand your financial goals
Ask yourself:

- Are you looking for monthly cash flow or long-term appreciation?
- Do you want passive income or are you comfortable being hands-on?
- Is this a short-term or long-term investment?

2. Run the numbers
Before renting, make sure the property makes financial sense:

- Monthly rent vs. mortgage payment
- Property taxes and insurance
- Maintenance and repair costs
- Vacancy allowance (5-10%)
- Property management fees (if applicable)

Side note: Your rent should comfortably exceed your total monthly expenses.

3. Check legal and zoning requirements

- Confirm local zoning laws allow rentals
- Review HOA rules (if applicable)
- Understand ladlord-tenant laws in your state
- Obtain any required rental licenses or permits
- Follow safety and habitability codes

4. Prepare the property

- Make necessary repairs
- Deep clean and refresh paint
- Ensure safety features are in place such as smoke detectors, carbon monoxide detectors, handrails etc.
- Consider durable flooring and low-maintenance finishes

5. Set the right rent price

- Review comparable rentals in the area
- Price competitively to reduce vacancy
- Balance market value with quality tenants

6. Screen tenants carefully

- Credit checks
- Employment and income verification
- Rental history references
- Background checks (where legally allowed)

7. Understand tax implications

Rental properties can offer tax advantages:

- Mortgage interest deductions
- Property depreciation

Repair and maintenance write-offs

Note: Always consult with a tax professional to maximize benefits.

8. Decide: Self-manage or hire a property manager?

Self-managing saves money but requires time.

Property manages handle:

- Marketing
- Tenant screening

- Rent collection
- Maintenance coordination

9. Plan for maintenance and emergencies

- Budget for repairs
- Build an emergency fund
- Have trusted contractors

So what are the benefits of converting a home into a rental?

They include:

- Monthly income
- Long-term appreciation
- Tax advantages
- Wealth building through leverage
- Flexibility to sell later or pass down generationally

Renting a home can provide wealth building for years to come. Not only can this be done on your current property, but an investment property as well. Matter of fact, many people become real estate investors and multiply this strategy to multiple properties, increasing their long-term wealth.

SECTION 6
BUILDING A LONG-TERM HOME WEALTH PLAN

6.1 Creating a 5, 10, and 20 Year Plan Improvement Roadmap

One of the smartest things a homeowner can do is create a long-term improvement plan for their home. Instead of reacting to repairs or making impulsive upgrades, a roadmap allows you to plan strategically, budget wisely, and increase your home's comfort, effiency, and long-term value.

A 5, 10, 20-year improvement roadmap helps you:

- Prioritize essential upgrades
- Spread costs over time
- Avoid financial surprises
- Maximize resale value
- Keep your home functional and modern

Let's break down how to build a practical long-term home improvement plan:

EVALUATE YOUR HOME'S CURRENT CONDITION

Start by assessing the major components of your home:

- Roof
- HVAC system
- Windows and doors
- Plumbing and electrical
- Foundation
- Kitchen and bathrooms
- Flooring and paint
- Landscaping and exterior features

Document the age, condition, and expected lifespan of each item. This becomes your planning foundation.

5-YEAR PLAN: MAINTENANCE, EFFICIENCY AND SMALL UPGRADES

Your focus should be on preventative maintenance, cosmetic improvements, and energy efficiency. This phase keeps your home running efficiently and prevents costly future repairs.

Typical 5-year projects:

- Interior painting
- Flooring replacement or refinishing
- Smart home upgrades
- Window replacements
- Basic bathroom refresh
- Appliance upgrades
- Landscaping improvements

Why does this matter?

Small improvements enhance daily comfort, boost energy efficiency, and protect your home from early deterioration.

10-YEAR PLAN: SYSTEMS, MAJOR UPDATES AND FINANCIAL IMPROVEMENTS

Your focus should be on structural systems and significant renovations. At this stage, you're addressing the major systems and high-impact upgrades.

Typical 10-Year Projects:

- HVAC system replacement
- Roof replacement
- Full bathroom remodel
- Kitchen remodel
- Electrical upgrades
- Plumbing updates
- Driveway replacement
- Deck or patio replacement

Why this matters:
These updates ensure your home stays safe, modern, and competitive in the real estate market. Always think resale.

20-YEAR PLAN: MAJOR RENOVATIONS AND LONG-TERM VALU GROWTH

Your focus should be on large-scale renovations and modernization. I call this future-proofing your home.

Typical 20-year projects:

- Full kitchen and bathroom remodel
- Home additions (if applicable)
- Layout redesign (Open concept updates)
- Major exterior renovation
- Aging-in-place upgrades

Why this matters:

These upgrades dramatically improve lifestyle, functionality, and long-term property value.

BUDGETING STRATEGY: SPREAD COSTS OVER TIME

Planning ahead let's you:

- Build dedicated savings
- Avoid emergency financing
- Time upgrades for best return on investment (ROI)
- Use seasonal contractor discounts (work could be less expensive in the off-seasons)

Create a home improvement savings fund and contribute monthly.

PRIORITIZE IMPROVEMENTS THAT ADD VALUE

Some improvements offer higher returns than others.

Some high-ROI Upgrades:

- Kitchen updates
- Bathroom remodels
- Energy-efficient windows
- Roof replacement
- Curb appeal improvements

Planning helps ensure you invest wisely, not emotionally.

BENEFITS OF A LONG-TERM IMPROVEMENT ROADMAP

- Reduces stress
- Eliminates surprise expenses
- Improves daily comfort
- Builds long-term equity
- Increases resale value
- Keeps your home modern

Think of your home improvement roadmap as a long-term investment strategy. When homeowners plan in 5, 10, and 20-year phases, they enjoy better living conditions today and stronger financial results tomorrow.

6.2 Protecting Your Home's Value

A home doesn't lose value overnight. It erodes. Small neglect can turn into expensive repairs. Roof issues become interior damage and poor drainage leads to foundation problems. Deferred HVAC maintenance becomes a $10,000 replacement instead of a $300 service.

To protect value we must:

- Schedule annual HVAC service
- Hire a roof inspector
- Clean the gutters
- Caulk and reseal around windows
- Have an expert look at the foundation and check for leaks

The market punishes deferred maintenance aggressively. Home buyers will assume the problems are worse than what they may seem.

Improvements that add value are:

- Kitchen and bathroom upgrades
- Energy efficient upgrades
- Functional layout improvements
- Exterior curb appeal

Throwing $80,000 into trendy finishes that date your home quickly is not protecting your value. Improve what buyers consistently pay for, not what impresses your friends.

Protect your structural integrity by adding stability to the foundation, improve the roof's condition, maintaining plumbing and electrical systems, and adding proper insulation and ventilation in crawl spaces and attics. When your structure is strong, your value will hold.

Being aware of your neighborhood is tied to your home's value.

You can't control everything, but you can:

- Stay involved in local zoning discussions
- Maintain property lines and boundaries
- Keep your landscaping looking sharp
- Support community standards

A neglected neighborhood brings down value.

Protecting value isn't just physical, it's also financial.

Never over-leverage equity, panic into a refinance, not understand comparable sales, and ignore local trends. Owners who monitor value annually are never blind-sided.
One uncovered disaster can erase years of appreciation.

Make sure you have:
- Proper homeowners insurance
- Umbrella policies when appropriate
- Documentation of upgrades made
- Flood coverage if relevant

Protection isn't pessimism. It's discipline.

What's the biggest threat to home value?

Short-term thinking.

Homes build wealth when owners:
- Stay consistent.
- Maintain standards.
- Upgrade strategically.
- Avoid emotional decisions during market dips.

The market has volatility. Well-maintained homes in solid areas recover. Neglected homes don't.

ROUTINE MAINTENANCE
Staying on top of routine maintenance on your home is one of the best ways to decrease the chances of a major issue creeping up on you. While It can be over-

whelming to think about maintaining a home, there are ways to make it less stressful. First and foremost, I recommend hiring a reputable home inspector to conduct a 'report card' of the home. A home inspection will provide details to areas that may need attention sooner than later. The inspection will also provide a starting point for you, so you don't feel lost in the process.

When I meet with a potential home seller, I always recommend they hire a home inspector to inspect their home before listing it. I do this because many times home sellers wait until a potential home buyer hires their inspector and surprises the seller with areas of concern. A seller should not be surprised by anything a buyer's inspector says. Having an inspection done, whether your'e thinking of selling or just wanting to learn the condition of your property, is sound advice.

PREVENTING MAJOR REPAIRS THROUGH SMALL UPKEEP

Preventing major repairs can be as simple as doing the little things that help avoid a major issue. From tuning up the furnace to cleaning out your gutters annually, you can avoid the big issues that come from neglect. If you take care of the small things, you can avoid costly issues.

Another great way to avoid major repairs is by having a home inspection. Having a home inspection will provide you with a full report card of how your home is doing condition wise. This report eliminates any surprise issues that may be lingering. A great home inspector will inspect all areas of your home, from attics to crawl spaces, every area will be graded. Before hiring an inspector, make sure to ask if they provide a full report with pictures of areas of concern. Never wait until a potential home buyer comes through with their inspector to know what the condition of your home is.

6.3 When To Reevaluate Your Plan Life Changes

LIFE CHANGES

Life changes can happen at a moments notice, or sometimes without notice. A new baby, a death in the family, a major repair issue, damage from a bad storm, a change in health, retirement, or any other type of life change that causes you to access your funds can cause a need to reevaluate your plan. Keep in mind it's not always a bad thing to review your plan on a regular basis. Never wait until an unexpected life change happens.

MARKET SHIFTS

Markets go up and they go down. It's important to know this and expect it. This is why your plan should be reevaluated more often than not.

INTEREST RATE OPPORTUNITIES

You should reevaluate your plan when the move in interest rates affects you. Don't react to chatter. React to math.

You should reevaluate when:

- You're within 1-1.5% of a refinance opportunity
- You're considering a HELOC (Home Equity Line Of Credit)
- You're thnking about upgrading or downsizing
- Adjustable rate reset is approaching

Consider this: A drop from 7% to 6.5% means nothing if you're locked in at 3%. However, a jump from 4% to 7% matters if you planned to make a move.

SECTION 7
THE MINDSET AND HABITS OF SUCCESSFUL HOME WEALTH BUILDERS

7.1 Thinking Like An Investor, Not Just a Homeowner

A homeowner will ask, "Can I afford this?" An investor will ask, "Is this the best use of my capital?" If you're thinking like an investor, you reevaulate your home wealth plan when returns, risk, or opportunity cost change.

Think about it this way:
1. Compare your home's return vs other options.
Calculate:

- Appreciation rate
- Equity growth
- Tax benefits
- Cost of debt
- Maintenance drag

Then compare it to:

- Market returns.

- Rental property returns.
- Business reinvestment.
- Paying down higher-interest debt.

If your primary home equity is earning 3-4% and other opportunities are realistically 8-12%, you need to question your allocation. Thinking like an investor and not just a homeowner will put you in the best financial situation possible.

UNDERSTANDING YOUR HOME AS A FINANCIAL ASSET

Most people either treat their home like an emotional trophy, or they treat it like a liability they hope goes up. An investor treats the home like a capital allocation decision. What do I mean? Let me break it down.

1. Your home is an asset, but a non-productive one.

Unlike a rental property, your primary residence:

- Doesn't produce income.
- Has carrying costs.
- Is not liquid.
- Is concentrated in one geography.

Its return comes from:

- Appreciation.
- Forced-savings (Principal paydown).
- Tax advantages.
- Leverage.

If appreciation + leverage outpace your carrying costs, it's working for you. If not, it's just an expensive shelter.

2. Understand your real return
Most homeowners overestimate their performance.

True return = (appreciation + principal paydown - maintenance - taxes - insurance - opportunity cost)

Opportunity cost in homeownership is about what you give up financially by putting money into a house instead of investing it somewhere else.

In simple terms:
Opportunity Cost = Return you could have earned elsewhere – Return you actually earn from the house.

Run this math over 5-10 years, not just last year.

3. Leverage is the hidden multiplier
If you put 20% down and the home appreciates 5%, your return on cash invested is far higher because you're leveraged.

Here's an example:
$500k home
$100k down
5% appreciation = $25k gain
That's a 25% return on your $100k before costs.
Leverage cost's both ways. When controlled, it's powerful.

Liquidity matters more than people admit. You can't

swipe your equity. If too much of your net worth is locked up in your house, you're equity-rich and flexibility poor.

Thinking like an investor means measuring:

- Equity-to-net-worth ratio.
- Cash reserves.
- Access to capital.

5. Your mortgage is either cheap capital, or dead weight.
Do you have a low fixed rate in a strong investment environment? Do you have a high rate choking cash flow? Time to reevaluate. Debt isn't emotional, it's math.

6. Exit strategy defines everything.
Ask yourself:

- Should I sell and downsize at retirement?
- Should I convert to a rental?
- Should I pass my home to my heirs?
- Should I use equity to fund investments?

If you don't know the exit, you don't know the strategy.

Here's something to consider.

For most Americans, their home is worth 60-80% of their net worth, their largest single asset, and their least analyzed investment.
This is backwards thinking.

Some people analyze a $10,000 stock position more than a $500,000 house.

If you want to think more like an investor, ask yourself these questions:.

Is my home:
1. Appreciating in a strong growth corridor?
2. Consuming too much capital?
3. Providing strategic leverage?
4. Aligning with my 10-20 year plan?

SEPERATING EMOTION FROM FINANCIAL DECISIONS

It's understandable to be emotional about a home because it's the place where you live, unless it's an investment property. If you don't control emotion, it will end up controlling your money. The good news is you don't eliminate the emotion, you build systems that override it.

Here's how disciplined investors seperate feelings from financial decisions:

1. Decide your rules before the moment

Emotion spikes during:
- Market drops
- Multiple-offer situations
- Rate hikes
- Big life changes

Create written rules when you're calm:

- I won't buy unless numbers hit X return.
- I won't sell based on headlines.
- I won't stretch beyond Y% of income.

Pre-commitment kills panic decisions.

2. Replace opinions with math.
Emotion says:
"This feels like a great deal".

An investor response is:

- What's the ROI?
- What's the cash-on-cash return?
- What's the worst-case downside?
- What's the opportunity cost?

Knowing the numbers reduces drama.

3. Seperate lifestyle from investment
Be honest with yourself. Are you buying granite countertops for ROI or ego? This line get's blurred the most when it comes to a primary residence. If it's lifestyle, own that. If it's investment, hold it to investment standards. Being confused here can be expensive.

4. Stress-test the downside
Emotion focuses on upside. Investors ask:

1. What if appreciation stalls?
2. What if income drops?
3. What if rates stay high?

If the decision still works under stress, it's rational.

5. Delay big decisions 24-72 hours.
Urgency fuels emotional mistakes, and you don't want that. If it's a real opportunity, it survives a pause. If it collapses under a pause, it was hype.

6. Define your long-term strategy
When your 10-20 year plan is clear, short-term noise loses it's power. Remember, emotion thrives in uncertainty. Clarity is stabilizing.

7. Get external perspective
Even sharp investors have blind spots. A good financial planner, CPA, or seasoned investor can challenge your thinking. They are not going to comfort you, but pressure-test you.

LONG-TERM THINKING VS. SHORT-TERM COMFORT
Here's some hard truth. Short-term comfort feels great. Long-term thinking builds wealth. They are rarely the same decision.

Let's explore short-term comfort (emotion-driven)
This is when the decision is about how it feels right now.

Here are some examples:
- Buying more house than you need because it "feels like success."
- Stretching your budget for nicer finishes.
- Refinancing to lower your payment but extending the loan back to 30 years.
- Not downsizing because you're attached to memories.

- Avoiding renting your home because "I don't want tenants".

Short-term optimizes:

- Status.
- Ego.
- Monthly payment relief.
- Emotional attachment.
- Convenience.

Emotion often ignores:

- Opportunity cost.
- Total lifetime interest.
- Equity efficiency.
- Liquidity risk.

Now let's explore long-term thinking (Strategy driven) This is when the decision supports your 10-20 year financial plan.

Some examples:

- Buying below your approval amount.
- Keeping a low-rate mortgage and investing extra capital.
- Downsizing to free up six figures in equity.
- Converting to rental for long-term cash flow.
- Selling in a peak cycle, instead of holding emotionally.

Thinking long-term optimizes:

- Net worth growth.
- Leverage efficiency.

- Tax strategy.
- Liquidity.
- Risk management.

It further asks:

- Does this move improve my balance sheet?
- Does this increase optionality?
- Does this align with my exit plan?

Some people get it wrong here because they call comfort an investment. They think a bigger house is a better investment. They think luxury upgrades equal a higher ROI. They think paying off the home early means an optimal capital allocation. Sometimes comfort is fine, if you consciously choose it. But if you think you're investing when you're really upgrading lifestyle, that's self-deception.

Here's an interesting question.

If someone offered you:

- The same home experience
- But $250,000 more in net worth 15 years from now

Would you take it?

If you answered yes, then some of your current housing choices may be comfort-driven.

7.2 Building Smart Financial Habits Around Homeownership

Most people treat their home like a place to live. Smart homeowners treat it like a long-term financial asset. The difference isn't income, it's habits.

Here are some tips on treating your home like an asset:

1. Buy based on strategy, not emotion

Excitement doesn't build wealth. Discipline does. Stay below your max approval amount, keep your total housing payment conservative, and always think resale from the day you buy. If the numbers only work when everything goes perfectly, it's a bad decision.

2. Protect your equity like it's a business

Your home equity is not a piggy bank for vacations and toys.

Smart habits include:

- Avoiding unnecessary cash-out refinancing.
- Tracking your home's value annually.
- Monitoring neighborhood trends.

Remember, equity is leverage-not spending money.

3. Reevaluate when the market shifts

Interest rates change. Property values shift. Tax laws evolve.

You should reassess:

- When rates move significantly.
- Every 2-3 years at minimum.
- When your income or life situation changes.

Passive homeowners drift. Strategic homeowners shift when needed.

4. Seperate comfort from investment

Granite countertops feel good, but will they return value when you sell? Before renovating, ask:

- Does this improve resale?
- Is this the standard for my neighborhood?
- Am I over-improving for my market?

Not every upgrade is an investment. Some are just consumption.

5. Maintain like an owner, not a renter.

Deferred maintenance destroys equity.

You should budget for these things annually:

- Roof
- HVAC
- Plumbing
- Exterior upkeep

Preserving your asset isn't optional. It's a must.

6. Keep liquidity

Being "house rich and cash poor" is financial fragility. Maintain 6 months of reserves, don't overextend on furnishings, and avoid draining savings for cosmetic upgrades. Liquidity gives you options. Options equal power.

7. Think exit strategy early.
Every home purchase should include an exit strategy, just like a business. Are you selling in 5-10 years? Are you going to convert your home into a rental? Are you looking to downsize later? If you don't know how you'll exit, you're guessing, not investing.

Homeownership builds wealth only when paired with discipline. Without smart financial habits, a home is just an expensive liability with a nice kitchen.

BUDGETING WITH INTENTION

Most people don't have a budgeting problem. They have a clarity problem. Budgeting with intention isn't about tracking every coffee you buy. It's about directing money toward what actually moves your life forward. Especially when you own a home.

Here's what that really means:

1. Start with outcomes, not expenses.
If you don't define where you're going, your money will drift. Ask yourself if you are paying your mortgage down faster, building reserves, saving for another property, or preparing to downsize in 5-10 years. Your budget should reflect your strategy without your impulses.

2. Give your housing costs a ceiling.
Just because you can afford a higher payment, doesn't mean you should.

Disciplined homeowners:

- Keep housing under control in comparison to their income.
- Avoid lifestyle creep when income increases.
- Increase savings before upgrading lifesetyle.

Freedom is better than spending too much on a home.

3. Seperate fixed, flexible, and future
Break your spending habits into three categories:

1. Fixed-Mortgage, taxes, insurance
2. Flexible-Food, dining, entertainment
3. Future-Repairs, upgrades, investments

Most people ignore future. That's why repairs feel like emergencies instead of planned expenses.

4. Create a home maintenance fund.
If you own property, repairs are not surprises. Budget between 1-2% of your home's value annually for the roof, HVAC, appliances, and exterior upkeep. This protects equity and prevents debt.

5. Fund opportunity.
Intentional budgeting creates margin. Margin allows you to refinance strategically, purchase an investment property, move quickly in a market shift, and/ or down-

size without pressure. Cash gives you options. Options give you power.

6. Review quartely, not just once a year.
Like I said earlier, markets change, rates move, and property values shift.

Ask yourself:

- Are you overpaying for insurance?
- Should you challenge your property taxes?
- Does refinancing make sense?
- Is your home still aligned with your goals?

If you don't control your money, your mortgage will control you. Budgeting with intention is about making sure your home serves your long-term wealth plan.

TRACKING EXPENSES AND IMPROVEMENTS

Tracking what your expenses are on home improvements can be daunting at first, however it's necessary to track everything to give you a better idea of what your expenses are. After all, how will you know how good or bad you are doing if it's not tracked.

PLANNING UPGRADES STRATEGICALLY INSTEAD OF EMOTIONALLY

Planning upgrades strategically is a sound decision to make so that you get the best ROI from your upgrade. In my career as a realtor®, I have met with many sellers who have not upgraded their home in years, sometimes none at all, and they are hoping for top dollar when they consider selling. Planning for upgrades helps your chance of getting more money when you sell.

7.3 Avoiding Common Emotional And Financial Traps

Most bad real estate decisions aren't caused by bad math. They're caused by unmanaged emotion.

Here's how to frame avoiding common emotional and financial traps around homeownership:

1. The "My home is worth more than the market says" trap.
Attachment inflates perception. You may be thinking that you raised a family there. You renovated the kitchen. You love the backyard. It's important to understand the market doesn't care.

In my experience with home buyers, they compare:
- Condition.
- Location.
- Comparable sales.
- Current rates.

When you overprice your home based on emotion, you:
- Risk your listing becoming stale on the market.
- Have to decrease the price to gain more attention.
- Weaken your negotiatiing power.

The longer your home sit's, the more leverage you lose.

2. The "Interest rates will come back down" gamble.
Waiting for perfect timing is speculation and rarely works. Yes, rates fluctuate, but life moves. Health changes, income shifts, maintenance costs rise, and property taxes increasing can all play a role in selling your home. Holding onto a property for the wrong reason can quietly drain wealth. So make decisions based on math and your life goals, not headlines.

3. The over-improvement mistake.
Upgrading for enjoyment is fine. Especially if you plan on living in the home long-term. But it's fantasy to think every upgrade you make equals an increase in value. For example, upgrading to a luxury kitchen when your in a mid-range neighborhood rarely pays off. High-end finishes in a starter home neighborhood is just as bad. Before renovating, ask yourself "Is this lifestyle spending or an investment decision?"

4. The "house rich, cash poor" problem.
Equity looks impressive on paper. But you can't pay your bills with paper gains. Some common issues involve not having emergency reserves, heavy credit card balances, and tapping equity for short-term consumption. Liquidity equals stability. Equity without liquidity equals stress.

5. Letting family pressure drive financial decisions.
This is common among seniors. Many will say:

- I don't want to leave memories.
- The kids want me to keep it.

- It's been in the family for generations.

Sometimes sentiment can override practicality.

If the home is too large, too expensive to maintain, becoming unsafe, or draining retirement funds, then holding onto it may be emotional comfort at a financial cost.

6. The fear-based freeze.
Some homeowners allow fear to get to them, causing them to not act at all.

They:
- Avoid valuations.
- Ignore maintenance.
- Refuse to view finances.
- Delay necessary transitions.

Inaction can feel safe, but stagnation can erode options.

7. Confusing comfort with security.
A familiar home feels secure. But true security is manageable expenses, a safe layout, strong reserves, and a clear exit strategy. Sometimes the bravest financial decision is letting go.

Here are some things to remember:
- Emotions are normal.
- Letting them dictate six-figure decisions is dangerous.
- The strongest homeowners seperate memory from market value, pride from pricing, and comfort from strategy.

KEEPING UP WITH THE NEIGHBORS

Keeping up with the neighbors, or commonly stated as keeping up with the Joneses, is financial sabotage. Especially in homeownership.

Some things to know:

1. Their income is not your income.
You don't know what they make, what they inherited, what debt they have, or what stress they hide. You're comparing your behind-the-scenes to their highlight reel.

2. Upgrading to impress others is expensive ego.
These are:

- New kitchen
- Bigger SUV
- Outdoor entertainment center
- FInished basement you hardly use

If the motivation is external validation, it's consumption. And upgrades based on ego hardly ever give you a high ROI.

3. Lifestyle creep kills wealth quietly.
Income goes up. Spending follows.
Instead of increasing investments, paying down principal, and bulding reserves, people upgrade to stay socially aligned. When comfort rises, freedom shrinks.

4. Debt becomes normalized.
When everyone around you looks upgraded, debt feels acceptable. But appearances lie.

Many "impressive" households are:
- Highly leveraged.
- Low on liquidity.
- One income disruption away from stress.

You never see that part.

5. It distracts from your actual goals.
Your neighbor's plan is not your plan. Maybe your real goals are early retirement, downsizing in 10 years, helping grandkids with college, or buying an investment property. Keeping up with others delays your own strategy.

6. Bigger isn't always better.
I am one to admit that I prefer a bigger home. But it's important to know that larger homes mean:
- Higher property taxes.
- Higher maintenance.
- More utilities.
- More cleaning.
- More complexity.

A bigger home could become a burden, especially later in life as you age.

7. Peace beats status.
True financial confidence is quiet. It's having manageable payments, strong reserves, strategic upgrades, and a clear exit plan.

So what's the bottom line?

The neighbors are not paying your mortgage. They're not funding your retirement. They're not covering your repair bills. If your decisions are influenced by comparison, you're not investing-you're reacting. And reaction can be expensive.

OVER-RENOVATING FOR PERSONAL TASTE

I'm a firm believer that while you live in a home, you should make it your own. With that said, every homeowner should keep resale in mind and avoid over-renovating a space, especially if it hurt's the value of the home. I know this can be hard to understand because you may be thinking of staying in the home for years, or even decades. I can tell you from experience in working with home sellers that more often than not, the home is not ready to sell because of areas that were over-renovated.

For example, if it's not common in your area to install granite countertops in the bathrooms, that could be money saved in your renovation. The same thought applies to fancy flooring. You never want to over-do it with upgrades.

So how do you find out what is hot and what's not in your area?

The answer is simple. Check out other homes on home websites and look through the photos. This is a great place to look before considering a renovation.

1. What types of countertops are in the kitchen and bathrooms?
2. What type of flooring is installed? What type of lighting fixtures are in the home?
3. Do they have light or dark colored paint on the walls?
4. Did a home sell for less money because it wasn't updated?

Being prepared and always thinking of the resale of your home will not only save you a ton of money, it will help sell your home faster and for more money when the time comes.

LIFESTYLE INFLATION AND OVERSPENDING

I shared a little about how overspending on a renovation can cost you thousands of dollars. Now let's talk about inflation as it relates to lifestyle.

7.4 Creating a Legacy Through Homeownership

A house alone is not a legacy. Equity mismanaged is not a legacy as well. An outdated will and a paid off home in probate is not a legacy either. Legacy through homeownership only happens when ownership becomes intentional.

Here's what this means:

1. Equity is a tool-not a trophy
Too many homeowners treat equity like a scoreboard. If your house went up $300,000, great, but now what?

A legacy mindset asks:

- Is the equity protected?
- Is it structured?
- Is it leveraged wisely?
- Does it reduce risk for my family?

If the equity dies with you in confusion, that's not legacy. That's cleanup work for your kids.

2. Ownership reduces generation struggle
Rent build's someone elses future. Ownership builds yours.

But the deeper truth is this:

When a family passes down a paid-off property, or even just significant equity, they pass down stability.

That stability:

- Reduces debt for the next generation.
- Gives heirs options to sell, rent, or refinance.
- Creates financial breathing room where opportunity is born.

3. Protection is part of the strategy
Real legacy planning involves:

- Proper titling (Trust, lady bird deed, etc.)
- Estate planning coordination
- Tax awareness
- Avoiding forced sales

If someone loses the house because planning wasn't done, ownership didn't create legacy. It created liability.

4. The emotional side and why this matters
Homes hold memories, represent discipline, and symbolize stability. But sentiment without structure is fragile. Legacy happens when emotional value and financial structure work together.

Creating legacy through homeownership can happen with proper planning and the information I just shared with you.

GENERATIONAL WEALTH STRATEGIES

Most people say "generational wealth" when they really mean to say is "I hope my kids get something." That's not a strategy. That's wishful thinking.

Here are real generation wealth strategies tied to homeownership and real estate.

1. Long-term property retention (Strategic hold, not accidental hold)

Families that build weatlh don't constantly churn real estate. They hold quality property long-term.

Why this works:

- Compounding appreciation
- Rent increases over time
- Debt get's smaller while value rises
- Inflation works in your favor

Consider this. One-paid off rental property can fund:

- College
- Provide retirement income
- Share down payments for the next generation

This is how quiet wealth is built.

2. Strategic use of trusts
Passing a home through probate is sloppy planning. Using:

- Revocable living trusts.
- Lady bird deeds (in certain states).
- Proper beneficiary structuring.

Keeps property out of court, reduces delays, and protects heirs from forced sales. If equity is tied up for a year or more in probate, opportunity is lost. Legacy requires structure.

3. Teaching financial literacy alongside asset transfer
This is where many families fail.

You can pass down a paid-off house, but if the next generation:

- Doesn't understand taxes
- Can't manage maintenance
- Overspends
- Refinances irresponsibly

The wealth disappears. Generational wealth is not just asset transfer. It's behavior transfer.

4. Leveraging equity without destroying it

There's a right way and a reckless way to use equity.

The smart way uses:

- Acquiring income-producing property
- Funding a business with a plan
- Strategic reinvestment

Dangerous uses:

- Lifestyle upgrades
- Consumer debt consolidation without discipline
- Serial cash-out refinancing

Equity should multiply, not evaporate.

5. Creating income-producing assets (Not just your primary house)

Primary homes build stability. Rental properties build freedom. A family that owns a primary residence, one or two cash-flowing rentals, has a dramatically different long-term trajectory than one that owns only one home. Income-producing property reduces reliance on jobs alone.

6. Insurance and risk protection
Generational wealth dies without protection.

Smart families:

- Carry adequate umbrella insurance
- Protect against liability
- Keep properties properly insured
- Avoid over-leverage

Wealth is built slowly and destroyed quickly. Risk management matters.

7. Clear succession planning
Ask these questions:

- Who get's what?
- How is it divided?
- What if one heir want's to sell and another doesn't?

A written, discussed, coordinated plan preserves both wealth and relationships.

Most middle-class families lose generational wealth within 1-2 generations, because there was no plan, the assets weren't structured, the next generation wasn't prepared, and lifestyle inflation consumed gains.

TEACHING FINANCIAL LITERACY THROUGH HOMEOWNERSHIP

Homeownership is the most reliable financial classroom most Americans will ever sit in.

Here's how to teach financial literacy the right way:

1. Start with the balance sheet-not the house
Most homeowners think:
My house is worth $400,000."

Financial literacy asks:
- What's the mortgage balance?
- What's the interest rate?
- What's the equity position?
- What's the monthly cost of ownership?

It's important to treat your home as part of a balance sheet:
- Assets
- Liabilities
- Net worth

Once others see that, they stop thinking emotionally and start thinking strategically.

2. Teach amortization
I would guess very few homeowners understand how a mortgage actually works.

Some questions to consider are:
- How much interest do I pay in the first 10 years?
- What does one extra principal payment per year do?
- How does refinancing change long-term cost?

When people see the math, behavior should change.

3. Connect equity to opportunity-carefully
Don't just say, "You have $200,000 in equity'"

Teach people:
- What happens if they sell.
- What happens if they refinance.
- What happens if they hold onto it.
- The tax implications of each.

Walk through each scenario to get a better understanding. People need to understand possible trade-offs.

4. Teach others the cost of impulse decisions
Here are some real world examples:
- Cash-out refinancing for lifestyle changes
- Overpricing a home and chasing the market down
- Skipping inspections
- Ignoring maintenance

Tie every mistake back to a financial consequence. Ownership magnifies financial behavior, good or bad.

5. Teach long-term thinking
Ask good questions:
- Where will this property be in 20 years?
- Could this become a rental?
- Is this home positioned to appreciate?
- What happens if one spouse passes away?
- Think foresight, not just the facts.

6. Bring estate planning into the conversation
I always recommend homeowners speak with an estate planner who can identify ways to set things up correctly. Some topics to talk about include titling, trusts, beneficiary designations, and probate. I would assume many homeowners have not had this conversation.

7. Make it practical, not academic
Don't lecture those you are trying to teach. Use real numbers, case studies, before-and-after examples, and hypothetical family scenarios. People learn when they see themselves in the example.

PASSING DOWN PROPERTY AND OPPORTUNITY
Passing down property and opportunity is not just about inheritance. It's about transferring advantage. Most families pass down 'stuff'. Few pass down structure.

Let's expand on this thought.

1. Property is stability
When a home is passed down properly, it gives the next generation something most people struggle for:

- No rent
- No mortgage
- Immediate equity
- Leverage for future moves

Housing is the largest expense for most families. Remove or reduce that, and you create margin. Margin creates opportunity. Without margin, people survive. With margin, they build.

2. Property creates optionality

Think about it. Opportunity isn't just living in the house. It's having options.

An inherited property can be:

- Sold to fund education.
- Rented for passive income.
- Refinanced to fund a business.
- Used as a stepping stone to upgrade.

The real gift isn't the house. It's the choices the house creates. When someone doesn't start at zero, their timeline accelerates.

3. Appreciation is silent wealth

Real estate compounds quietly.
A home bought decades ago often represents:

- Massive appreciation
- Inflation protection
- Locked-in low costs

When that transers properly, the next generation benefits from decades of discipline they didn't have to start from scratch building. That's leverage across time.

4. Structure determines whether opportunity survives

Here's the uncomfortable truth.

Many inherited homes get:

- Forced into probate.
- Sold under pressure.
- Divided in conflict.
- Mismanaged.

Without proper planning (trusts, correct titling, clear instructions), property becomes a burden instead of an advantage. Passing down a property without planning is like handing someone a toolbox without instructions.

5. The behavorial component

You can pass down a paid-off home. But if the next generation doesn't understand taxes, maintenance costs, treats the equity like a spending account, or fights over control, the opportunity evaporates. Generational wealth fails more from behavior than market conditions. Real legacy planning includes proper education.

6. Emotional capital matters too

Homes hold memories and delightful stories. They represent sacrifice, discipline, and stability. When framed properly, passing down property communicates "We built something. Now build further". That psychological headstart is powerful. Kids who grow up seeing long-term ownership think differently about money.

Let's end this section with a valuable question:
"If something happened to you tomorrow, would your home create opportunity, or confusion?"

SECTION 8
WHEN OWNING A HOME DOESN'T LEAD TO WEALTH

8.1 Homeownership isn't always beneficial

Throughout this book you have learned all the ways homeownership can lead you to wealth, and in some cases, financial freedom. From purchasing the right property to investing your built-up equity. But like anything else, with pro's there are con's. I would not be doing anyone any favors if I left out the reasons why owning a home may not lead you to wealth. So let's dive into the reasons why wealth may not happen.

- **High maintenance and repair costs** — Roof replacements, furnaces, plumbing issues, and ongoing upkeep can quickly eat into any appreciation gains.
- **Property taxes and insurance keep rising** — Even after the mortgage is paid off, homeowners still face recurring expenses that can strain finances over time.
- **Homes are not always appreciating assets** — Real estate markets can decline or remain flat for years depending on the area and economic conditions.

- **Interest payments add up** — Over the life of a mortgage, homeowners may pay tens or even hundreds of thousands in interest alone.
- **Limited liquidity** — Unlike stocks or savings, home equity is not easily accessible without selling or borrowing against the home.
- **Lifestyle inflation** — Some homeowners continually upgrade furniture, landscaping, remodeling, and décor, creating ongoing spending habits instead of building savings.
- **Unexpected life changes** — Job loss, divorce, medical expenses, or relocation can force a sale at the wrong time financially.
- **Opportunity cost** — Large down payments and monthly housing expenses may prevent investing in retirement accounts, businesses, or other wealth-building assets.
- **Overbuying a home** — Purchasing more house than you can comfortably afford can lead to debt stress and little room for saving.
- **Transaction costs are expensive** — Realtor commissions, closing costs, taxes, and moving expenses reduce profits when selling.
- **Poor financing choices** — Adjustable-rate mortgages, cash-out refinancing, or repeated borrowing against equity can weaken long-term financial growth.
- **Neighborhood decline or market shifts** — Changes in schools, crime rates, local employers, or development can negatively impact property values.
- **Homeownership can create a false sense of wealth**

— A home may increase in value on paper, but unless equity is converted into usable assets, it may not improve overall financial security.

- **Retirement challenges** — Some homeowners become "house rich but cash poor," with most of their net worth tied up in the property but limited income available for daily living.

It is important for you to understand these risks and how they can resent themselves because not every investment is a sure thing. WIth this said, I believe there are more benefits than risks when owning a home.

CONCLUSION

RECAP: EQUITY AS A POWERFUL PATH TO WEALTH

In this book, we covered a lot of areas on how you can build wealth through homeownership. In section 1, we covered how to choose the right property, negotiate effectively, and apply strategy when choosing financing. In section 2, we covered what home equity is and how it works, how it grows naturally and intentionally, and the role of market appreciation. I shared with you the tools and methods you can use to estimate your home's current value and when you should get a professional to come up with a valuation.

In section three you learned what refinancing is, what a rate-and-term refinance is vs a cash-out refinance, and when you shouldn't consider a refinance. We also explored how refinancing can build wealth by lowering monthly payments, which can increase your savings, and shorten loan terms to build your equity faster. You also learned how to avoid making mistakes when refinancing by understanding closing costs, and comparing multiple lenders and what they have to offer. In section 4, I shared with you the renovations that provide you the highest return on investment, focusing on kitchens and bathrooms because those are the best rooms to renovate, as well as adding curb appeal to your property. We also dove into effective flooring, paint and lighting improvements. We talked about cost-efficient updates in regards to windows and door enhancements, HVAC and water heating upgrades, renewable and smart home upgrades and why these updates matter. I shared with you the projects that rarely add value to a home, such as over-customizing, adding a pool, converting bedrooms into specialty rooms, and high-end landscaping with high maintenance. I stressed the importance of knowing the market, working with the right real estate professionals, and budgeting and planning tips.

Section 5 covered long-term wealth building, how home values tend to trend upward, historical appreciation examples, and why patience is key. I shared how you can use home equity loans to fund improvements, fund additional investments, and apply to retirement strategies, provided you don't over-leverage. We further discussed paying off your mortgage strategically by making bi-weekly payments, applying extra payments towards principal, and the benefits of paying down your mortgage vs. investing your money elsewhere.

In section 6 we covered the importance of creating a 5, 10, and 20 year plan by evaluating your home's current condition, making a plan for home maintenance, efficiency, and making small upgrades. We further discussed protecting your home's value through routine maintenance, seasonal checklists, and preventing major repairs through small upkeep. I shared the importance of reevaluating your plan often, especially if life changes, market shifts, or interest rate opportunities occur.

In section 7, I covered the mindset and habits of successful home wealth builders. Understanding your home as a financial asset, seperating emotion from financial decisions, and long-term thinking vs. short-term comfort. I shared building smart financial habits by budgeting with intention, tracking your expenses and improvements, and planning upgrades strategically instead of emotionally. You learned how to avoid common emotional and financial traps from trying to keep up with the neighbors, over-renovating for personal taste to overspending and adjusting for lifestyle inflation. Lastly, you learned about creating a legacy through homeownership through generation wealth strategies, becoming more financially literate, and passing down property and opportunity.

ENCOURAGEMENT TO TAKE ACTION

It takes alot of courage to take that first step toward a future of financial abundance and long-term wealth. Furthermore, it takes action. The information I shared with you in this book will guide you towards making smart, confident decisions that take you to where you want to go. Implementing what you learned and leaning on the expertise of other professionals in their field is a great way to make the decision to take action and move forward. Remember, knowledge is not power by itself, but knowledge mixed with action equals power. The power to build wealth from homeownership.

Seasonal checklists

Seasonal home maintenance checklists help homeowners stay proactive, rather than reactive. By addressing routine upkeep throughout the year, small issues can be caught early. This can prevent costly repairs, preserve your homes value, and protect your long-term equity.

These checklists provide a simple, organized approach to maintaining a home efficiently while supporting smarter, more intentional homeownership over time.

The following are a series of checklists seperated by season.

Spring Checklist

Exterior & Yard

- Inspect roof for missing, loose, or damaged shingles
- Clean gutters and downspouts; ensure proper drainage away from foundation
- Check siding and trim for cracks, rot, or peeling paint
- Inspect foundation for cracks, or signs of water intrusion
- Power wash siding, walkways, decks, and driveways
- Inspect deck or patio for loose boards, railings, or nails

- Reseal deck, fence, or concrete if needed
- Trim trees and shrubs away from the house and roof
- Check exterior caulking around windows and doors

Doors & Windows

- Inspect weatherstripping and replace if worn
- Check window screens and repair or replace damaged screens
- Clean window tracks and test operation
- Re-caulk windows and doors as needed
- HVAC & Mechanical Systems
- Schedule HVAC spring tune-up (AC system)
- Replace HVAC air filters
- Clean vents and registers
- Inspect outdoor AC unit; clear debris and vegetation
- Check attic ventilation

Plumbing

- Inspect for leaks under sinks and around toilets
- Check water heater for corrosion or leaks
- Test sump pump (if applicable)
- Inspect outdoor faucets and irrigation system
- Look for signs of slow drains

Electrical & Safety

- Test smoke and carbon monoxide detectors
- Replace batteries as needed
- Inspect outdoor lighting and replace bulbs
- Check GFCI outlets in kitchens, baths, and exterior

Interior

- Inspect ceilings and walls for water stains or cracks
- Clean ceiling fans and reverse direction for warm weather
- Deep clean carpets and flooring
- Check attic and basement for moisture or pests
- Declutter and organize storage areas

Summer Checklist

Summer Home Maintenance Checklist Exterior

- Inspect roof for loose, cracked, or missing shingles
- Clean and inspect gutters and downspouts
- Check siding, brick, and trim for damage or peeling paint
- Power wash siding, walkways, decks, and patios
- Inspect driveway and walkways for cracks; seal if needed
- Repair or replace damaged screens on windows and doors
- Check foundation for cracks or signs of water intrusion

Cooling & Energy Efficiency

- Schedule air conditioning system service
- Replace or clean HVAC filters
- Clean outdoor AC condenser coils
- Check thermostat operation (upgrade to smart thermostat if needed)
- Seal air leaks around doors and windows
- Close blinds or install UV-blocking window treatments
- Inspect attic ventilation and insulation

Plumbing

- Check outdoor faucets and sprinkler heads for leaks
- Inspect irrigation system and adjust watering schedule
- Look for leaks under sinks and around toilets
- Flush water heater to remove sediment
- Check sump pump and drainage systems

Safety & Systems

- Test smoke detectors and carbon monoxide alarms
- Inspect fire extinguishers
- Clean dryer vents to reduce fire risk
- Check electrical outlets and outdoor GFCIs
- Inspect garage door operation and safety sensors

Outdoor Living & Landscaping

- Trim trees and shrubs away from roof and siding
- Inspect deck, patio, and railings for loose boards or rot
- Seal or stain deck and outdoor wood surfaces
- Clean grill and outdoor cooking areas
- Check fencing for damage or loose posts

Storm & Weather Prep

- Secure outdoor furniture and umbrellas
- Inspect drainage around the home to prevent flooding
- Check seals around windows and doors
- Review homeowners insurance coverage for storm damage

Fall Checklist

Exterior & Structural

- Clean gutters and downspouts; ensure water drains away from foundation
- Inspect roof for missing, curled, or damaged shingles
- Check flashing around chimneys, vents, and skylights
- Seal cracks in siding, brick, or stucco
- Touch up exterior paint or seal exposed wood
- Inspect foundation for cracks or moisture issues
- Store or secure outdoor furniture and equipment

Windows, Doors & Insulation

- Inspect caulking and weatherstripping; replace where worn
- Check for drafts around windows and doors
- Install storm windows or doors if applicable
- Add door sweeps to reduce heat loss
- Check attic insulation depth and coverage

Heating & Fireplace

- Schedule professional furnace or boiler inspection
- Replace HVAC air filters
- Test thermostat and replace batteries
- Clean air vents and returns
- Inspect fireplace and chimney; schedule chimney cleaning if used
- Check carbon monoxide detectors and smoke alarms

Plumbing & Water Systems

- Disconnect and drain outdoor hoses
- Shut off exterior water valves (if available)
- Insulate exposed pipes in unheated areas
- Drain and winterize sprinkler systems
- Check water heater for leaks and proper operation

Electrical & Safety

- Test all GFCI outlets
- Inspect extension cords and replace damaged ones
- Check exterior lighting for shorter daylight hours
- Replace batteries in smoke and CO detectors
- Yard & Drainage
- Rake leaves away from foundation and drains
- Trim trees and branches away from roof and power lines
- Aerate lawn and apply fall fertilizer
- Clean and store lawn equipment
- Check grading to ensure water flows away from home

Garage & Storage

- Lubricate garage door tracks and test auto-reverse feature
- Organize and safely store flammable materials
- Inspect weather seals around garage door

Winter Checklist

Exterior

- Inspect roof for missing or damaged shingles
- Clean gutters and downspouts to prevent ice dams
- Check siding and trim for cracks or gaps
- Seal exterior cracks with caulk or weatherproof sealant
- Shut off and drain exterior faucets; store hoses
- Inspect chimney and cap for damage or blockages
- Clear walkways and driveways; keep ice melt on hand

Heating & Energy Efficiency

- Schedule furnace or boiler inspection/service
- Replace HVAC filters
- Test thermostat (consider a programmable or smart thermostat)
- Seal air leaks around doors and windows
- Add or check weather stripping
- Insulate exposed pipes and attic spaces
- Reverse ceiling fans to clockwise for heat circulation

Plumbing

- Insulate exposed pipes in basements, crawl spaces, and garages
- Check for slow leaks or drips
- Keep cabinet doors open in extreme cold to allow warm air circulation
- Know how to shut off the main water valve

Fireplace & Safety

- Have fireplace and chimney professionally cleaned
- Check damper operation
- Inspect fire extinguishers
- Test smoke detectors and carbon monoxide alarms
- Replace batteries if needed

Interior

- Check attic insulation and ventilation
- Inspect basement for moisture or drafts
- Clean dryer vents to reduce fire risk
- Check sump pump operation
- Look for condensation on windows (sign of poor insulation)

Emergency Preparedness

- Stock emergency supplies (flashlights, batteries, blankets)
- Keep snow shovel and snow blower ready
- Service generator if applicable
- Review home insurance coverage for winter-related risks

CONNECT WITH JASON GELIOS

REALTOR® and **Senior Real Estate Specialist** (SRES®)
Jason Gelios is a licensed Michigan REALTOR® and Senior Real Estate Specialist serving the Southeast Michigan region. He represents home buyers and sellers in achieving their real estate objectives with professionalism and integrity. In addition to residential sales, Jason assists clients with short-and long-term rental needs and provides services to real estate investors throughout the area.

ON THE INTERNET
Jason's website, ***JasonGelios.com,*** is a wealth of information, advice, and videos. Also the main hub for the ***AskJasonGelios Real Estate Show***.

AskJasonGelios Real Estate Show
Weekly episodes uploaded to the major social media networks including YouTube. Special guests drop by of-

ten to share valuable advice too!
Visit ***www.JasonGelios.com*** to subscribe for free.

AskJasonGelios Real Estate Show PODCAST
Available on the go wherever you listen to your podcasts. Jason Gelios shares valuable home buyer, seller and homeowner tips. Subscribe and listen today!

ON SOCIAL MEDIA
Jason shares valuable information regarding real estate tips and home maintenance tips on his social media outlets.

YouTube: Search 'Jason Gelios'

Facebook: https://www.facebook.com/jasongeliosrealtor/

Twitter: https://twitter.com/jasongelios

Instagram: https://www.instagram.com/jasongelios/

Pinterest: https://www.pinterest.com/jasongelios/

LinkedIn: https://www.linkedin.com/in/jasongelios

PUBLIC SPEAKER
Jason speaks at local home buyer events, senior communities and other venues offering home buying, selling and homeowner tips to participants.

MONTHLY E-NEWSLETTER

Subscribe to Jason's free monthly e-newsletter titled ***Homeowners Update,*** sharing tips from home maintenance to real estate knowledge.
Visit ***www.JasonGelios.com*** to subscribe for free.

AskJasonGelios Show WEEKLY EMAIL

Don't miss out on new episodes of the ***AskJasonGelios Real Estate Show***! Sign up for a weekly email with the latest episode plus other great content.

AUTHOR

Jason Gelios is the author of **Think Like a Realtor**, a practical guide to navigating the buying and selling of residential real estate with confidence and clarity.

He also wrote the motivational self-help book **Beating the Force of Average**, which shares proven strategies to rise above mediocrity, achieve the success you desire, and create the life you truly want.

For readers age 55 and over, Jason authored **The Seniors Guide to Buying and Selling a Home**, a real estate book tailored specifically to the unique needs of older adults.

Get your copy today on Amazon!

www.ingramcontent.com/pod-product-compliance
Lightning Source LLC
LaVergne TN
LVHW022044200926
848481LV00003B/774
* 9 7 9 8 2 3 4 1 2 9 7 9 6 *